Linkeain

For

Business

Consultants

Debra Faris

Linkedin for Business Consultants
Published by
Solutions Press
Newport Beach, California

© 2018 Debra Faris
ISBN: 978-0-9996497-2-5
All rights reserved

This is a work of non-fiction. The ideas presented are those of the author alone. All references to possible results to be gained from the techniques discussed in this book relate to specific past examples and are not necessarily representative of any future results specific individuals may achieve. Information presented is correct to the best knowledge of the author at the time of publication.

The author of this book has no connection of any kind whatsoever with LinkedIn Corporation or any of its subsidiaries or allied companies. LinkedIn Corporation has given no endorsement of the strategies outlined in this book, implied or explicit.

Contents

Author Index

Introduction

In today's world, where things are so easily, instantly obtainable on the Internet, it's necessary to bring back old-world traditional relationship-building. *Linkedin for Business Consultants* was crafted to teach executives and entrepreneurs the necessary skills to build long-term relationships with the right people through networking, engagement, and follow-up.

In addition, this book will teach them the entrepreneurial and leadership skills necessary to develop "an eye for opportunity." They will develop their underlying intuitive skills, which are the basis of all human connections, enabling them to build productive, long-term relationships that will shape their destiny.

LinkedIn for Business Consultants is for executives, entrepreneurs and anyone who wants to leverage LinkedIn for what's next in their business opportunities in a rapidly changing world. Social media has gone from being social to your sharpest tool for business adventures. LinkedIn can help you find new clients and connect with like-minded people to network with and build relationship currency.

LinkedIn has more than 400 million members and is more than a rolodex. This unique book shows you 12 strategies from how to leverage the one million groups to finding the perfect charity to make a difference. Check out the incredible stories and how they are using LinkedIn.

Acknowledgements

Thank you to all the people who were instrumental
in helping create this book:

My first book was dedicated to my son Phil Godwin, who wanted
to be an anthropologist. Thank you for your love & your spirit that
will forever be a part of me. Phil's girls, Denise his wife and babies
Scarlet & Sophie, I'm so blessed to have you be his love to light up
are hearts. Gina, my daughter, I never knew someone could be as
smart as they are beautiful, and August takes after his mommy in
every way. Dan my son, thank you for our family dinners. They
keep me appreciating the little things.

Thank you, all the people who have influenced
and contributed to my life.

Lee Pound, you are the whole enchilada; a brilliant
writer, grammatical king, patience of a saint, work
ethics of a Thomas Edison, support like a Dallas
Cowboys cheerleader, instincts like a

Aggie, I can't recommend you enough for your 25
years of knowledge to how to put the pieces together
from hotel to speakers. For people looking for a great
planner, you are the one!

Karen Taylor Roane, You are one of a kind. Lee and I
can't thank you enough. You are truly a blessing to all
of our authors to put the shine in shining stars.

Chapter 1
What's my purpose on
LinkedIn?

People who use time wisely spend it on activities that advance their overall purpose in life.
--John Maxwell

Why LinkedIn?

Facebook, Twitter, Google+, Instagram, LinkedIn, Pinterest, Tumblr, Flickr, Meetup; the list goes on and on. Social media sites are cropping up left and right on the internet and are here to stay. People interact and connect on social media sites, forming virtual communities and networks, sharing information and ideas. With all these choices, why use LinkedIn?

You may think social media is only for people chatting endlessly about personal details, gossip, or sharing recipes and photos. What difference can it make for you? Isn't social media is for young people? The answer is simple. LinkedIn is about building relationships and deep connections. In business, you built relationships both online and offline with your fellow co-workers, professional associates, recruiters, even competitors. You can deepen these relationships by connecting with them on LinkedIn. Then you expand your connections and relationships using LinkedIn. You build a team of connections and relationships that will help you in the future as you search for a new opportunity.

Although relationships and connections are important in general, they are far more critical for those who find themselves in transition. The best way to find a job is through connections, both who you know and who knows you. When you build a team of individuals

1

who know you, like you, and want to help you; you make finding the right job far easier. LinkedIn is the perfect place to start. When you build your business profile, you are building your future business persona. People begin to learn what you're all about.

Singleness of purpose is one of the chief essentials for success in life, no matter what may be one's aim.
--John D. Rockefeller, Jr.

Start now! In today's competitive job market, you cannot afford to be left behind. All professionals need to use and become experts at LinkedIn, the sooner the better. Building profiles that represent who you are, show your authenticity and character, and showcase your talents and awards will give the business world a glimpse of what to expect as they review your profile.

You have a track record of experiences and successes that you need to share, so the world knows who you are and what you can do. LinkedIn is your tool for spreading that message. Its members' names appear at the top of Google search rankings because it has more than 400,000,000 members, massive traffic, and constant change in content. It even outranks websites people have paid tens of thousands of dollars to create. This gives you a big advantage when potential employers or customers search for you. In addition, LinkedIn's wide range of privacy options allows you to control what others see about you.

I call LinkedIn your mini-website because it gives you many of the same benefits as having your own website. You can connect and build relationships, get your needs shared, and showcase your skills and talents.

LinkedIn offers many avenues to create and discover your ideal job or future clients. That's why I suggest you build your profile in three parts.

1. First, complete the basics and develop a "complete" profile on LinkedIn.

2. Second, design your profile so that busy executives and top recruiters can read it easily.

3. Third, show your personality and your connection with the real world in a way that gives you high credibility and attracts the right people to you.

Even though LinkedIn is designed as a way for business owners, executives, and professionals to connect, do business, and find jobs, it is still social media. Many people think it is enough to put up their profiles, which are all about themselves, and expect to attract the people they want without interacting. This is the wrong approach. To get from point A to point B with potential connections, you must communicate with them. Business is all about talking with people, creating connections, and building communities. To succeed on LinkedIn, you must create engagement and partake in or even create your own community.

When a client of mine says, "I thought this wasn't social media," I say, "That's what I thought in the beginning, too. Then I found out

I was wrong and became very excited about the opportunities the site offered."

When you see these opportunities, you will think, "Oh My Gosh, Gold, Gold, Gold, Gold!" LinkedIn is the most phenomenal site I have ever seen. That's because you get tons of free publicity with your LinkedIn profile.

Once you get started, you will build an edge over your competition for the best positions now available or soon to emerge. But you must approach it as you would any other serious professional representation of your business persona. This book will take you through all the steps.

When I chased after money, I never had enough. When I got my life on purpose and focused on giving of myself and everything that arrived into my life, then I was prosperous.
--Wayne Dyer

Whether or not you have already decided to jump into LinkedIn, this book will show you how to get it done right and make your best professional impression. LinkedIn is a unique channel that gives the consumer multiple dimensions and tons of value, all for free. It has no hosting fee and no monthly membership fee (although members can pay for an upgrade account which gives a few perks and extra benefits).

Be sure to ask yourself these questions. What is your intention on LinkedIn? Is it to find a job or connect with known associates? Is it to find groups that can help you market your products or services? Is your network going to be online or offline or both? Identify the people you want to meet and the message you want to send. Then connect, follow up and be part of the communities that keep you connected.

LinkedIn is recognized for their influencers. We have added a few of our own.

John C. Maxwell

Leadership Expert | Trainer of 6 Million Leaders | Certification Program For Coaches, Teachers, Speakers & Professionals

West Palm Beach, Florida Area | Professional Training & Coaching

Current	The John Maxwell Company, "A Minute With Maxwell" free video series, Christ Fellowship Church
Education	Ohio Christian University

Send a message ▼   500+
                                    connections

My Influencers: John Maxwell

In my first book, which was for college students, I started off with one of my first mentors, Mike Ferry, who is one of the most powerful influencers in the real estate world for Realtors for over 30 years. The average agent earns $6,000 a year. Mike has made more millionaire agents than any other trainer coach, probably in the world. Mike holds training events that 3,000 people attend to change the way they do business and make more money.

Back in 2003, I was at a seminar with 20 different leadership speakers, who were known as game changers. But I was particularly intrigued with one...John C. Maxwell, who has sold over 25 million books that have impacted business professional, entrepreneurs and people who want to make a difference. At that time, John's super popular NY Best Seller was *Becoming a Person of Influence* (Co-Author Jim Dornan). We all know money isn't everything; however, through the years, many influencers seem to have a lot of the same character traits and are also financially successful. John spoke of leaving a lasting legacy through creating relationships that last through the test of time.

> *Without love, there can be no connection, no future, and no success together.*
> **--John Maxwell**

John came from the belief that if you treat every person as if they were the most important person in the world, they are somebody to you. Coming from connection with the intention that you value them naturally creates a leader people will want to follow. This created a transformation in businesses, with a mind-set more about making a difference than a competitive attitude of everyone-out-for-themselves. United we stand, separately we fall. So it is critical to partner with like-minded people while being purposeful.

Over the years, I kept what I had learned from John in mind as I pursued my own career. He was a real-world influencer who made a difference.

When the digital world of social media opened up, I expected John to show up there as well. LinkedIn came to dominate the business professional community. When I heard that they had decided to create a way for people to follow leaders by naming 500 Influencers every year. I started checking on my favorite influencers. When I found Dr. Maxwell on LinkedIn, I was surprised to learn that he has trained more than 6 million leaders, was a recipient of the Mother Teresa Prize for Global Peace, worked with leaders from the Luminary Leadership Network, and spoke at most of the Fortune 500 companies and sold 25 million books.

Consider adding him to your influencer list.

Online and Offline - EHarmony

The most successful online, offline internet communication vehicles are in the infamous dating world led by companies like EHarmony and Match.com, which allow their members to seek relationships that fit their criteria, ranging from friendships to dating to meeting someone with whom they can spend their rest of their life. LinkedIn works in a similar fashion except it is centered in the business world. You connect with other members, build relationships, and use those relationships in your career.

Each time you look at LinkedIn and its members, you will find people that interest you and people you want to connect with. Maybe someone shared how they accomplished goals in a specific position, or maybe the groups they joined might interest or benefit you.

These are all ways to connect with other human beings. You can also see employment histories, where people started and how their careers advanced through the years from, for example, a copy clerk to Senior VP of the Western Region for a billion-dollar company. As you continue to search and explore, you see life and careers from a different perspective.

You can incorporate your offline connections in LinkedIn as well. Connect with your family, friends, and business colleagues as you build your network. Since you already have a relationship with these offline connections who are like you, start with them. Then as you continue to work, add the connections you make during these events to your profile. That will build your online connections and build your bucket. Expand your profile as you expand your life. Don't underestimate any connection. Sometimes one odd connection can lead to a great job. Use LinkedIn to foster both your online connections and your offline connections. Build your networks and develop relationships that help you accomplish what you desire.

Authenticity and Transparency

Building an authentic profile on LinkedIn requires skill and evaluation. To show people who you really are, you need to dig into your character traits, values, and skill sets and make sure that the image you're painting for viewers represents you. The more authentic you make your profile; the more value your connections will have to you. You only get one chance to make a first impression. Be true to yourself and allow your readers to get a feel for who you are.

At a Tony Robbins seminar many years ago, the three most important things I learned were to know your purpose, know your intention, and that questions are the answer. I got off track many times, slowed down, collected myself, and started to ask better questions, which led to better results. Nobody can change your results for you. You are the only one who can change your life and you do it by asking, "What results did I get and how could I do it differently to get better results?"

We will receive not what we idly wish for but what we justly earn. Our rewards will always be in exact proportion to our service.
--Earl Nightingale

Einstein said, "If you keep doing the same thing over and over, you will keep getting the same result. That's called insanity!" This is why questions are the key to a powerful LinkedIn profile.

You may ask, "What if my job experience isn't that exciting?" You are more than just your job experience, so, in a following section, I want you to ask, "Who Am I?" which will begin your journey on your new path.

Shifting Your Mindset

It is important to know your mission and purpose for connecting on LinkedIn before you start. If you start with the end in mind, setting up your profile and making important connections will create a more effective message.

Know why you're on LinkedIn and what you want to accomplish before you start, and your outcome will be aligned with your goal.

Mindsets are beliefs about yourself and your most basic qualities. Think about your intelligence, your personality and your talents. Are these qualities fixed traits that can never be changed or are these traits that you can change and cultivate throughout your life?

There are two basic types of mindsets, fixed mindset and growth mindset. A person with a fixed mindset believes that their basic traits are fixed qualities that they cannot change. With a growth mindset people believe that their most basic abilities can be developed through dedication and hard work.

So, you ask, how does this relate to LinkedIn? The mindset that you approach LinkedIn with will dictate your results. Just like life, if you approach LinkedIn without understanding all its dimensions and details and don't use its flexibility, you will wind up with results different than you expected. Those who think they can set up a pretty profile and that people and jobs will flock to them automatically are sure to be disappointed.

When you approach LinkedIn, remember it is a mindset connecting with others and building relationships. Mike Ferry™ teaches a course called *Mindset, Skills, Action, and Motivation* that shows people how all of these components work together for success. You start with the right mindset and the rest falls into place. If you approach LinkedIn with the mindset and strategy of knowing where you want to go, who you need to meet, and ask the right questions as you build your profile, you will find LinkedIn to be a valuable tool in your networking.

I once shared a story about my skydiving adventure with a CFO (chief financial officer). He said, "Who would jump out of a perfectly good airplane?" That was his mindset. He wanted to keep his feet on the ground.

I said, "I understand why you might feel that way. But I did it, you didn't. Wouldn't you like to know what I learned from it?"

Even if you never plan to jump out of an airplane, you can still benefit from the knowledge I gained and how I felt. Everyone has their own mindset. Sometimes it benefits you to take on someone else's mindset or at least share their experience, so you can learn from it.

When I finished, my friend/client said he didn't realize he was looking through such a narrow perspective and that he would have missed possibilities for collaboration. He is a left-brain expert, analytical and detailed, where I have a creative, exploratory, communicative, curious side; therefore, when we collaborate, we bring added value, whether in a company or a relationship.

Who Am I? I am...!

Who am I? Have you ever sat in your room on a quiet Sunday afternoon and pondered that question? You know your name and what city you came from and what you look like. But when you really get right down to it...Who am I? And once I figure out who I am, how do I tell everyone else?

Early in their careers, many people are quick to pick a field and jump in without thinking about their passions and without taking time to outline their desires and visions.

When this happens, a progression of jobs creates a career and before we know it we are in our early fifties, burned out, unhappy with what we're doing, and living unfulfilled lives.

To succeed, you must learn the truth of who you are. The famous Greek philosopher, Socrates, said, "Know Thyself." This is one of the deepest truths in life. You must know who you are before you can achieve a happy, fulfilled life.

Man masters nature not by force but by understanding.
--Jacob Bronowski

People don't understand the significance of the many bits and pieces that make up their lives. They think one job was a waste of time or didn't benefit them or that a boss was too harsh. Later in life they realize that everything they ever did made them the people they are today.

For instance, early training in honor, trust and integrity followed you as you moved into responsible positions such as Manager, Director, CEO or CFO. Past opportunities create benefits for an individual's future, because in the end it's all about your character.

You need to portray your character in your LinkedIn profile; because if you do it correctly you will send a powerful message to the people you want to connect with. Identify key character traits that describe you and incorporate them into your profile. The more your profile reflects your genuine self in an authentic and transparent way, the more chances you have of connecting with the audience you desire. You need to find keywords that identify who you are, what you like, and what you want. You will recognize these words when they resonate with you. If you think about the word for more than five seconds, it belongs in your profile. Keywords that resonate with you and describe who you are create an in-depth LinkedIn profile that will attract the people you want to connect with as you continue in your professional career.

The next questions you need ask are: What are the goals of your connections? What are your goals for the communication you will have with people on LinkedIn? What are the goals of the communities you are part of?

Make a very clear statement that says, "Here's who I am and here's who my clients are." If you are in finance, write down all those characteristics, print out profiles of about 100 other financial people, and highlight all the things that resonate for you.

People may hear your words, but they feel your attitude.
--John Maxwell

When you ask yourself these questions, you begin to think about the message the people reading your profile are receiving. What does your profile communicate about you and how will your audience interpret that message? If your message isn't clear to you, it won't be clear to them. Put yourself in their position; think like your recruiter. Does your profile show off your talents, strengths, and accomplishments? If not, fix it! This is your opportunity to brag about yourself. If you're not confident doing that (a lot of us aren't), have a friend read your profile and ask for their input. Listen as they brag about you; include their words in your profile. You're amazing and everyone deserves to know about you!

Ensure that you read your profile once you have completed it and that it conveys the correct message in the correct tone. You want to attract people to you and increase your chance to build relationships. If your profile is poorly worded or unattractive, it may cost you the jobs, orders, business, relationships, or closeness that you want. You only get one chance to make a first impression. Make your profile shine and shout out your greatness.

I am Big Bird

I love documentaries. One night as I was scrolling through Amazon, I saw *I am Big Bird* and thought it was a little kid's movie, but it turned out to be the real-life story of Jim Henson and Caroll Spinney, who was one of the original puppeteers on the Muppets on Sesame street. We often miss the biggest part of LinkedIn, which is that if we don't know who we are, how are others supposed to like us, know us and trust us.

Know thyself.
--Socrates/Plato

This extraordinary movie is about how the writers wrote a part for Big Bird but the part they wrote didn't fit the human actor Caroll Spinney's personality. They tried and tried but the actor and part refused to work. Spinney told his lifelong friend to pick someone else who could do the part. Jim refused to let him quit.

Then he gave Spinney the script and dressed him up as Big Bird and suddenly the part worked. Spinney went on to turn that role in a 30-year career, an amazing piece in history.

Here are This Chapter's
Business Consultant Influencers

As you read these profiles, look for possible referrals for your needs. .

Is there something in their story you connect with?
Could you gain a new idea or insight for your business or career?
Who do you know or who do they know that can help both of you?
If you needed help or wanted to buy a product, what would it be?
How do you follow up when you meet someone?
When people view your profile, how do you want them to feel?
Do your tribes line up so you could be Power Partners?
What are your favorite questions to ask in an introductory call?

Steve Rodgers

Alchemy Advisors
Where Accountability & Leadership
Meets Success

"Breaking through resistance is the price you pay for the dream you say you want." ~ Steve Rodgers

I was a rebellious teenager who moved out of my house when I was only 17, barely graduated high school, went on to learn from different education sources and self-development to eventually become a Warren Buffet CEO of a 25-Billion company using many of the principles outlined in "Think and Grow Rich."

My wife and I lived after a near-death experience which eventually led me to discover my true and highest purpose in life which is Coaching & Consulting C-Suite Executives, Companies and Teams to find, maximize and increase their highest good & purpose in life & business. I specialize in understanding & maximizing the inner workings of companies to help them increase their value proposition to the consumer and find ways to increase their profits. I also help professionals transitioning into becoming an entrepreneur or making the best of the journey once they are on the path. And most importantly, I help my clients discover the best ways for a company or individual to create more happiness, joy & fulfillment in business and life!

C-Suite Executives, Companies and Teams. Executive Consulting, Coaching, Workshops

▶ Become More **P**roductive

▶ Garner More **P**rofit

▶ Experience More **P**urpose

▶ Be of Service to Others, become a Servant Leadership Minded individual

SPECIALTIES: Consulting, Coaching, Public Speaking, Training, Acquisitions /Merger, Marketing & Internet Expertise, Franchise & Branding Knowledge, Start-Ups, Creating Raving Fan Customers, New Business Models, CEO & Executive Leadership Expertise, Real Estate, Mortgage

What will you do differently this year from last year or what do you want more of? This year it is important that my focus is even more keyed on growing my international speaking business and fine tuning my ideal client to make a perfect match for us both

Who now is a Mentor, Coach or Strategist that is on your advisory council? Mark Thompson is a good friend and amazing advisor to me. He has worked with the great leaders like Charles Schwab, Sir Richard Branson, Steve Jobs, and many companies like Pinterest, Linkedin, World Bank and more.

What discipline could someone learn from you? The discipline to know what to positively transform so you can evolve to your highest good!

On what topic at parties would you really like to "get into it"? My deepest conversations and most enjoyed are what is your "true purpose" , why are you here on the planet and are your truly doing your life's work? If yes tell me more and if not tell my why.

When "winning someone over" do you think facts or emotions carry the day? Emotions always seem to rule our decision-making process, influence our heart and help guide us in our best paths. Love the saying "the sound understands what the mind can't conceive"

If there were one problem in the world you could solve, what would it be? Acceptance. Everyone wants to be loved and accepted.

Steve's Favorite Characteristics

Driven, Knowledgeable, Open, Creative, Resilient, Results Oriented, Ultra Positive, Purpose Driven, Insightful, Calm, Joyful, Problem Solver, Intuitive, Fearless

Steve Rodgers aka *"The Transformational C-Suite Coach"*
"Transition-Transform-Evolve"
♕ Premier C-Suite Executive Coach & Consultant ♕ Accomplished International Speaker & Best-Selling Author ♕ Proven Transformational Expert ♕ Business Development that Drives Profit
♜ steve@steverodgerstoday.com ☎ 858-829-2969 ♕
www.theAlchemyAdvisors.com ✓

Rosalyn Kahn

International Tedx Speaker~
Speaker Coach ~Life Coach~
Author~Executive Speaker~
Working With United Nations

"You never know by the words you say whose life you can change."
~ Rosalyn Kahn

Being diagnosed with scoliosis at age 13 was not only a challenge but an opportunity. I learned the lens of an outsider as a teenager which was counterbalanced with a fundamental shift in mindset to success. This included becoming most valuable varsity swimmer, moving from pain to success, landing on TEDx, to unveiling others' greatness. Human relations to sales, teaching, training has gifted me with keys to human interaction.

Today I inspire individuals to tell their unique story in their authentic voice. Everyone has a gemstone inside with their personal journey. My gift is to help unveil that story, to tailor a talk that will mesmerize the audience to hang on your every word and drive them to reach their desired results.

▶People don't know how to choose a topic and craft a speech that will reach the audience they desire. I coach them to refine their knowledge and passion into a speech that resonates with the audience they want to reach. Then they speak with power on the topic their audience needs to hear.

▶Authors have no idea how to present their ideas effectively or sell their books by speaking from the stage. I teach them to face their fear of speaking so they can publicize their important message from the stage to large audiences and magnify the reach of their books.

▶Business owners need to stand out from their competitors. I train them to use public speaking to establish instant credibility and expertise in their specialty and attract customers & clients they can reach no other way.

SPECIALTIES: Writing speeches, Speaking, Coaching Speakers, Teaching, Training, Producing Seminars, Speech editing, Author, coach, Storytelling, Researching, Artist, Reducing Stress

What movie touched you by its meaning or inspired you? The movie Forrest Gump impacted me the most. On one of the most critical turning points in my life was when it seemed out of control. A former student sent me a box of chocolates and stated the line, "Life is like a box of chocolates, one never knows what they might get."

If you could be anyone for a day, who would it be and what experience can you envision? I would be a world leader who teaches how to achieve peace by opening our minds to the other person's perspective. We gain a lot from using empathy to understand them.

What discipline could someone learn from you? The power of storytelling. When you create a story, you introduce the setting, identify the characters, show what they want, and determine the message the story imparts to the audience. They learn how to take action to reach their goal.

What subject or argument most stirs your emotions, why? Do the right thing. I often face questions like, "What do I do?" "What do I say?" A huge part of me always says, "Do the right thing." I want to help my students do better, save a student from harm, prevent a person from committing suicide. I want you to understand me because I am your friend.

In helping others, is it better to teach them, give them, or show them? Life is a combo meal. There are four types of learner; auditory, visual, auditory/writing and kinetic. It depends on the individual which one you would use. I teach people speaking through listening to me. I show them papers to illustrate what is desired. Students learn gestures, remember the sequence, and watch speeches to critique and become better speakers.

Rosalyn's Favorite Characteristics

Compassionate, Charismatic, Loyal, Intelligent, Integrity, Enthusiastic, Gratitude, Meticulous

Rosalyn Kahn aka: "Master the Message with Passion & Purpose"

M.A. ♘ Strategy ♟ Speaker ♟ Business Growth ♟ BUSINESS ALIGNER ♟ RELAUNCHING BUSINESS ♚ Consultant ♚ Business Coaching ♚ Corporate Executive ♚ Educator ♚ Trainer

♜ kahn.rosalyn@gmail.com ♟ 818-583-7328 ♛
http://www.rosalynkahn.com

The Starfish Story

An old man was walking on the beach
one morning after a storm.

In the distance, he could see someone
moving like a dancer.

As he came closer, he saw that it was
a young woman picking up starfish
and gently throwing them into the ocean.

"Young lady, why are you throwing starfish
into the ocean?"

"The sun is up, and the tide is out, and if I do not
throw them in they will die," she said. "

"But young lady, do you not realize that there are
many miles of beach and thousands of starfish? You
cannot possibly make a difference."

The young woman listened politely, then bent down,
picked up another starfish and threw it into the sea.

"it made a difference to that one."

Adapted from the original
by Loren Eiseley

Chapter 2
Get Started with Your Story

Life is a gift, and it offers us the privilege, opportunity, and responsibility to give something back by becoming more.

--Tony Robbins

Tony Robbins ⬚fluencer

#1 New York Times best-selling author, life and business strategist, philanthropist, entrepreneur

San Diego, California · Professional Training & Coaching

Current   Anthony Robbins Holdings, Inc.

1,542,011
followers

My Influencers: Tony Robbins

We all have a story. Our stories are about how we've connected with people throughout our lives. Life has its hurdles. At some point, we all struggle with something, whether it is the loss of a job, a death in the family, or a broken heart. Sometimes, bouncing back isn't easy.

I looked for people who had amazing stories like billionaires Tony Robbins, Richard Branson, Bill Gates, and J.K. Rowling, who have had their world crumble at some point in time. The way they reacted to that crumbling is what made them great!

My first event with Tony Robbins was over 30 years ago. My mother had committed suicide. My entire world fell apart. I was confused. I lost my focus and my faith. I felt like a bird with a broken wing. I had to take things one day at a time while I found the right people to guide me on my path. I knew it would take knowledge, skills, and time to put the pieces back together.

An old yet proven adage says that when the student is ready, the master (or teacher) will appear. Well, I was ready, and Tony Robbins' messages resonated with the core of my being.

I spent 10 days in Hawaii at Tony's Mastermind learning how to change my state, learning that my language created the feeling of being stuck by repeating an old story that no longer served me. I also found that Questions are the Answer. By asking better questions, I would get better answers, ultimately leading me to my desired results. It was the most game-changing event I had ever attended. I will forever be grateful to all the extraordinary leaders in the world that Tony shared with us at this cutting-edge event. They became role models of excellence for us and taught us their success principles of tenacity, perseverance, focus, and discipline.

"It is by going down into the abyss that we recover the treasures of life. Where you stumble, there lies your treasure."
-- Joseph Campbell

Life's journey is rarely a straight line. It has curves, forks and ruts. When people talk about stories, the most famous mythologist is Joseph Campbell, whose mentor was Carl Jung. He described the legendary Hero's Journey, and showed how it mirrored a human's life journey. The Journey, with its three segments of Separation, Initiation and Return, is at the core of almost every movie script written today.

My favorite movie is *Wizard of Oz*. Dorothy is wishing she was somewhere else when by coincidence a giant tornado sweeps her away to a land far far away, where she finds three fellow journeyers, Scarecrow, Tin Man and Cowardly Lion. Dorothy tragically almost dies several times before they reach the Emerald City and find a funny little man behind a curtain pretending to be a mighty wizard who helped her understand that all she ever wanted was already right there at home and all she had to do to get there was click the heels of her ruby-red slippers twice.

When you get lost, follow your yellow brick road to your mentor to find your way home.

Character isn't something you were born with and can't change, like your fingerprints. It's something you weren't born with and must take responsibility for forming.
--Jim Rohn

Your Story: Use your imagination like JK Rowling

"Imagination is more important than knowledge, for knowledge is limited to all we now know and understand, while imagination embraces the entire world, all there ever will be to know and understand," Albert Einstein said.

When it comes to your resume or your LinkedIn profile, you want to write like J.K. Rowling. *Harry Potter*, Rowling's most famous work, was all imagination. Use your imagination like she did.

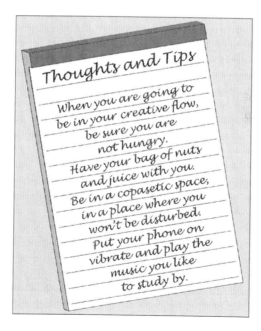

Thoughts and Tips

When you are going to be in your creative flow, be sure you are not hungry. Have your bag of nuts and juice with you. Be in a copasetic space, in a place where you won't be disturbed. Put your phone on vibrate and play the music you like to study by.

Rowling gave us the idea of calling a regular human a "Muggle" and wrote the novels from the perspective of wizards. Look at your resume on LinkedIn from the perspective of the wizards (your recruiters and connections). You don't want to be viewed as an ordinary "Muggle" but want to be chosen to receive on your 11th birthday, like Harry, the letter accepting you into Hogwarts School of Witchcraft and Wizardry. Lily's sister Petunia lived an ordinary lifestyle, but Lily did not. Lily was accepted into Hogwarts while Petunia was not. Portray yourself as the person recruiters are looking for. Use words in your resume that draw recruiters to you.

Rowling created the amazing wizard Dumbledore, who could see through to who a person truly is. Dumbledore knew when he was just a student at Hogwarts that Tom Riddle was evil to his core. Many years later Tom became Voldemort. Dumbledore could read your LinkedIn Profile and see straight through to the real you. He could tell if your description is just pieces of your resume hashed into the LinkedIn Profile.

Not everyone is like Dumbledore. You must show who you truly are in your description of yourself. Your connections will not read between-the-lines because they are not Dumbledore. Present yourself as if you were trying to get Snape to see who you really are, not the pretentious person he considers you to be because he knows who your father is. Who you choose to be will convince the Sorting Hat to place you in Gryffindor and not in Slytherin.

Appearances can be deceiving, but they do matter. No one thought Neville Longbottom would become a hero. He appeared to be the dorky outcast who was never good at spells. In the end, Neville Longbottom stood up against Voldemort when everyone thought Harry was dead. Over time, we learned that the actor who portrayed Neville was a very handsome young man.

This story shows that appearances can be deceiving. In the beginning no one expected much from Neville, but he surprised everyone when he turned the Boggart from Snape into Snape in his grandmother's clothes. Don't let your appearance make people believe in you less. Let your picture show who you are and what you can do. Appearances are everything, just as Snape was terrifying to

Neville but became a person to laugh at in his grandmother's clothes. You can change the way others perceive you by changing your profile picture on LinkedIn.

Think of your connections as your wand. The wand chooses the wizard, according to Ollivander. Your connections choose you, but they don't do everything for you. The wand doesn't make the magic but is a channel for the magical spells to be made.

Your connections are the same. Whether you choose your connections, or they choose you, you need to master your connections to produce the end result you want. That end result is like severing a connection with the Avada Kadavra spell or lighting your way with a Lumos spell. If you don't use your connections, they will do nothing for you. If you learn to master the craft of connecting with people, they will carve a path for you in the darkness like a Lumos spell does.

A Picture is worth a Thousand Words :)

This phrase is widely attributed to Frederick R. Barnard, who published an article, *One Look is Worth a Thousand Words*, in *Printer's Ink* in December 1921 on the effectiveness of graphics in advertising. He attributed the phrase to "a famous Japanese philosopher" although he later admitted he made up that origin and that he hired a calligrapher to put it into Chinese characters in the 1920s (see image below).

Even given this somewhat sordid history, the phrase does point out an important truth. The first forms of written language developed from a series of pictographs, first the ancient Egyptian hieroglyphics, then the cuneiform script of the ancient Sumerians. The ancient sailing merchants, the Phoenicians, then created the first known alphabet from these pictographic scripts.

Even before alphabets, ancient cave dwellers used images to convey important information with drawings of floods or men hunting mammoths on cave walls. Use of images has always been deeply entrenched in the human experience.

As time passed, the importance of the image to civilization has not changed and will never change. We as humans use our sight to make decisions about what to wear, what we will eat, where we will sleep, and who we will be attracted to.

This is why the images you use on LinkedIn are so important. If you have no picture, people may think less of you. If your picture is unprofessional, it might turn them off. A visitor will look at your picture and decide in 10 seconds if they want to know more about you. In those first 10 seconds, you must make your great impression that invites people to check you out.

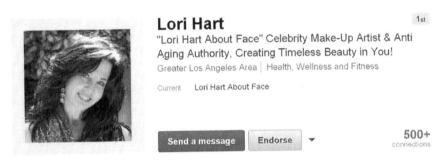

Lori Hart   1st
"Lori Hart About Face" Celebrity Make-Up Artist & Anti Aging Authority, Creating Timeless Beauty in You!
Greater Los Angeles Area | Health, Wellness and Fitness

Current   Lori Hart About Face

Send a message   Endorse ▼   **500+**
                                    connections

In networking and business, you need to play the part. If you play golf with a business partner or meet a new client at the driving range, you don't wear a suit and tie, even if you are a finance industry professional who wears a suit and tie to the bank every day. On the golf course, you would wear a polo shirt and Bermuda shorts or a golf t-shirt and a pair of khakis. You wouldn't wear a suit to play on a Saturday night, but you would wear a suit to meet the HR Manager when applying for a job.

Many times, you only have one instant to make a good impression on LinkedIn (and in life). How do you do that? You need a picture that fits as seamlessly into your profile as a window frame melds into a million-dollar house. Your picture shows who you are in your industry. When your picture doesn't fit expectations, you give your viewers a sometimes unconscious sense of unease.

Not all people use a simple head shot. I've seen people in full baseball gear in their profile pictures to show they are a coach. Remember that this is only good in moderation. Too much creativity can give mixed signals to your viewers.

Success comes from taking the initiative and following up... persisting... eloquently expressing the depth of your love. What simple action could you take today to produce a new momentum toward success in your life?
--Tony Robbins

Always keep your photo as clean and simple as possible. The background in some pictures can be distracting. It is better to pose outside by a tree than use a fake generic background like a pretend beach with a beach ball, because truth creates the vibrations that attract people to us. Use a background that best represents your industry, but is not too busy.

You don't have to use a traditional studio and pay a lot of money to get a good portrait. Today's smart phones have high resolution cameras and make it easy to upload a profile picture in just seconds.

A great photo will include: a hairstyle that shows your face; clean, pressed, and appropriate clothes that fit the part; and a smile, one that appears as if you are looking at them though the camera lens.

The best advice I can give you is to look at hundreds of pictures on LinkedIn in the industry that you are considering.

When you upload a new picture, LinkedIn will share it with your connections. If you have several photos you like, switch them out every once in a while. You never know who might see your new photo and whether it might be the trigger that gets them to refer you to the person who is looking for someone just like you in your industry!

Character is Everything

Things aren't always how they appear There are 3 million hoarders in the United States. You would never know most of them had this problem if you them at a party or worked with them in an office. Our trajectories can lead us in different paths and we never know how many ways we can help someone.

Brian Scudamore built a $150 million empire with his company 800 Got Junk, starting with only $700 because he wanted to help these people clean up their lives. Knowing your character traits helping others with their self-worth or business are ways to find your niche..

A am fascinated by how organizers and a company called 800 Got Junk transformed people's lives by helping them create new spaces and lifestyle choices.

Throughout this book, at the end of each chapter I will share my mentors and their characteristics. Below is a list of some character traits. Find five or six that express who you are. As you progress through the book, find other mentors and explore their traits. When it comes to great qualities in other people, as John Demartini says, "You can't see something in others that you don't see in yourself."

As we said in the "Who am I" section, you can use these character traits to reflect your skills in the specialties section and in your summary. Remember, some of these can be used again as your SEO keywords. Thread some of your character traits in your skills section.

Formatting: Start with the end in mind

The formatting in the Summary section is critical. You must create easy-to-read snippets that even a busy CFO will read. If the eye can't see the full picture, the visitor to your profile will flip to the next profile. Many things have changed with LinkedIn just like life evolves every day. In the beginning LinkedIn wanted people to put contact info in a designated section, but now it is common pract74ice to put your name and information at the top of the summary. I like to make sure it is in this more prominent position at the top of the summary.

Key Character Traits

Accountable	Adaptable	Adventurous
Alert	Ambitious	Appropriate
Assertive	Astute	Attentive
Authentic	Aware	Bravery
Calm	Candid	Capable
Certain	Charismatic	Clear
Collaborative	Committed	Communicator
Compassion	Comradeship	Connected
Conscious	Considerate	Consistent
Contributes	Cooperative	Courageous
Creative	Curious	Dedicated
Determined	Diplomatic	Directive
Disciplined	Dynamic	Easygoing
Effective	Efficient	Empathetic
Empowers	Energetic	Enthusiastic
Ethical	Excited	Expressive
Facilitates	Fairness	Faithful
Fearless	Flexible	Friendly
Generative	Generosity	Gratitude
Happy	Hard Working	Honest
Honorable	Humorous	Imaginative
Immaculate	Independent	Initiates
Innovative	Inquiring	Integrates
Integrity	Intelligent	Intentional
Interested	Intimate	Joyful
Knowledgeable	Leading	Listener
Lively	Logical	Loving
Loyal	Manages Time Well	Networker
Nurturing	Open-Minded	Optimism
Organized	Patient	Peaceful
Planner	Playful	Poised

Polite	Powerful	Practical
Presents Self Well	Proactive	Problem Solver
Productive	Punctual	Reliable
Resourceful	Responsible	Self-confident
Self-generating	Self-reliant	Sense of Humor
Sensual	Serves Others	Sincere
Skillful	Spiritual	Spontaneous
Stable	Strong	Successful
Supportive	Tactful	Trusting
Trustworthy	Truthful	Versatile
Vibrant	Warm	Willing
Wise	Zealous	

SEO: What is it and how does it help you?

LinkedIn is your own personal mini-website. It gives you the opportunity to advertise yourself and connect with many people. To use it most effectively, you must pay attention to Search Engine Optimization.

Use your headline (or tagline) as your advertisement. This is a powerful key to getting recruiters, human relations representatives, and positive connections interested in you. The words in your headline are a billboard with keywords that attract people to you.

Keywords are gold. They are the words you want to be known by and known for. When you get clear on whom you are your words provide clarity about the job or position you are seeking. For maximum impact, use keywords that people are searching for.

John Chow is one of the top bloggers in the world. People don't look for him by name; they just want to find a blogger. It doesn't matter how many hits you get; it doesn't matter how many connections you have.

LinkedIn Heading & Summary

Your Name
Header   {SEO Keywords}
Current Position   {Search Engine
                       Optimization}
Previous Position

Summary Section:

Name & aka...
Slogan or Tagline
Email Address & Phone#
Website Address

Two blank rows

Your history
(no more than 5 lines)

Two blank rows

Today I am...
three lines

Two blank rows

► **P**roblem

One blank row

► **A**ction

One blank row

► **R**esults

Two blank rows

Your specialties,
two lines

It only matters what SEO words you use, because that is how the people you want to attract will find you. John Chow put every blog and writing word that you could think of in his header, his profile description, and his past experiences because that's how people will search for him.

Also use the current meaning of old words. For instance, content is the new word for writing, so recruiters looking for writers may search for content as well. You can also use other similar words such as writing, writer, and editor because some people might not search for content, but they might search for writing. In another field, instead of using market plans, I could use the word "launches." The goal is to hit some keywords people might embed in longer search phrases. If your simple keyword or two brings your profile up when a longer phrase is typed in, you will succeed in getting found.

To keep the attention of your connections, reword your header from time to time. When you edit your header, even just by a few words, the change shows up on the timeline of all your connections. That keeps you visible at the top of the search pages.

For keywords and SEO, find the words your future competitors use for their industry. As you work on your social media, spend 15 minutes to look at the profiles of these potential competitors. In each of the seven sections, the Heading, Summary, People also Viewed, Skills and Endorsements, Recommendations, Groups, and Companies They Follow, you will find the keywords they use. Note and use these words as you create your LinkedIn profile.

Here are This Chapter's Business Consultant Influencers

As you read these profiles, look for possible referrals for your needs.

Is there something in their story you connect with?

Could you gain a new idea or insight for your business or career?

Who do you know or who do they know that can help both of you?

If you needed help or wanted to buy a product, what would it be?

How do you follow up when you meet someone?

When people view your profile, how do you want them to feel?

Do your tribes line up so you could be Power Partners?

What are your favorite questions to ask in an introductory call?

"Stop thinking, start writing." ~ Lee Pound

I first discovered my love of writing in high school, when I joined the staff of the school newspaper. My early career as a newspaper editor for 15 years honed my writing skills. Twenty years as Chief Financial Officer in the magazine business and as a seminar promoter honed my business skills. Writing 12 books of my own and coaching dozens of writers to publication built my training and teaching skills.

Today I coach and train business owners to become published authors. If you can talk, you can write. Inside every one of us is a book, short or long, that can make a difference to your readers, your clients, and your world. Your book will make you the recognized expert in your field and will attract your ideal clients

▶ Find your book idea through a series of coaching questions.

▶ Mold your idea into a focused emotion-based narrative that will keep your readers reading.

▶ Market your books and ideas to the readers who most need to read them.

SPECIALTIES: ★Writing / Editing / Speaking / Coaching Writers / Teaching / Producing Seminars / Publisher★

★Line Editing / Book writer / Author coach / Technical writer / Book layout / Fiction / Storytelling / Non-Fiction★

What discipline could someone learn from you? The ability to act instead of thinking too long. The key to great writing is to create a first rough draft that you can then refine and improve.

Who in your childhood was a major influence that helped shape your life? Two very important persons. My father, Ray Pound, who gave me a sense of adventure and the knowledge that nothing was impossible as well as a role model for running a business. My high school coach, John Tynes, who showed me that you didn't have to be a star athlete to participate in sports and that I could be a successful, confident adult.

When "winning someone over" do you think facts or emotions carry the day? If you can't connect on an emotional level, you will lose the sale, the reader, and the client. Even those who say they want facts have a secret emotional point that you must touch to win.

In helping others, is it better to teach them, give them, or show them? The highest level is to train. Right repetition creates mastery. Showing does little if there is no follow-up, teaching lasts only a short time (how much high school history do you remember), and giving devalues the knowledge you have to share (if it costs nothing, how good can it be?).

If there were one problem in the world you could solve, what would it be? People talk past each other, not with each other. Communication cannot happen until both parties agree to understand the other on a deep level even if they still disagree.

What will you do differently this year from last year or what do you want more of? I am concentrating on training writers through my CSL Writers Workshop. My passion is to help people enhance their communication skills, so they can influence people who need to hear their message.

Lee's Favorite Characteristics

Caring, disciplined, inspirational, adventurous, fairness, generosity, intuitive

Lee Pound, The Write Coach

Writing a Book will Build Your Expertise,
Boost Your Business & Change Your Life!
▶ 949-246-8580 ▶ Lee@LeePound.com ▶ www.LeePound.com ▶
wwwCSLWritersWorkshop.com

There is so much gray to every story – nothing is so black and white.

~ Lisa Ling

A defining moment in my life occurred in 7th grade. I wanted to attend a violin music camp and my parents requested an excused absence. He denied my request, and we were told that if I had requested a week off to go deer hunting it would be excused. My parents and I remained steadfast in telling the truth and I took an unexcused absence. Integrity matters, and I also knew at that moment that I would lead a creative life.

Today, I create authentic, people-oriented advertising content. It begins with brand strategy and written messaging. My integrated, multi-platform philosophy includes producing and hosting podcasts and digital video productions. After all, there are different ways to tell a tale.

► Consultants and coaches need to connect with people. This is beyond networking, it's making an emotional connection with potential clients. I shape success stories that reinforce your professional expertise.

►Digital video is the most powerful medium and you should be incorporating it into your business. It doesn't need to be an extravagant production, but a handheld video "selfie" with bad audio might not present you or your brand in the best light. Remember, perception is reality.

►Podcasts are perfect for relaxed conversations describing your business philosophy, client successes, and personal information. They provide personal insights to the listener who can join in anytime, anywhere. I love interviewing and learning from people.

SPECIALTIES: Authentic Marketing Content/ Storytelling/ Copywriting/ Brand Strategy/ Digital Video/ Podcasts/ Panel Moderator, Conference Host.

What movie touched you by its meaning or inspired you? I was impressed by the *Dunkirk* movie and saw it twice. Beyond the epic and heroic story, each physical element of air (Spitfire dogfights), land (beach battle sequences), and sea (boats on the English Channel) were characters unto themselves. You felt as if you were in the film, not watching it.

Who in your childhood was a major influence that helped shape your life? Every summer, professional actors and musicians from New York City came to my community to perform classic summer stock musical theater productions. I was in many musicals, which opened my world and changed my perspectives beyond the confines of small town agrarian life.

Who now is a Mentor, Coach or Strategist that is on your advisory council? I recently had the genuine pleasure of meeting Master Business Coach, Danny Creed. His wealth of experience and approach to personal improvement resonates quite deeply with me. Plus, we get along as if we've known each other all our lives.

What discipline could someone learn from you? Execution. Great ideas are worthless without it.

What subject or argument most stirs your emotions, why? Labeling genuine news reports as fake news. Being in the media, I know this is a form of propaganda that has taken root worldwide as it has in other dark periods of human history. Each must respond with facts and speak truth to power.

In helping others, is it better to teach them, give them, or show them? As president of AMA Los Angeles, I've had the pleasure of assisting the Los Angeles Ronald McDonald House in teaching them video marketing strategies. This way, they can learn and produce their own videos as they are a powerful medium for fundraising.

Philip's Favorite Characteristics

Creative Integrity Networker Reliable Resourceful Sense of Humor Vibrant
Philip, AKA the Connector. Create Content. Connect People™
Great ideas are worthless without execution.
▶ philip.tish@gmail.com ▶ 310.614.0155
▶ www.gottastory.com ▶ Twitter: @PhilipTish
Find Philip on Facebook, LinkedIn, and Refer.com and where ever goods are sold. Gotta Story? Lemme Tell It!™

Connections

As the word connection echoes,

It travels through the universe
in vibration it hopes to touch

One Human,

One Life,

One Living Thing,

That in its Connection

It will Experience

That it too exists

Debra Faris

Chapter 3
Click, Click, and Connect

The only limits in our life are those we impose on ourselves.
--Bob Proctor

Bob Proctor
Chairman / Co-Founder at Proctor Gallagher Institute
Scottsdale, Arizona | Professional Training & Coaching

Current Proctor Gallagher Institute, The Secret, LifeSuccess Publishing
Previous Nightingale Conant Corporation
Education Universidad del Salvador

Send a message ▼

500+ connections

My Influencers: Bob Proctor

Connection... Connection... Connection... Everywhere we go, we see reference to "connections"; from billboards to TV commercials. It's perhaps one of the top ten most commonly used words. It is a buzzword all across different media, but trail blazers have been spreading seeds of its inspiration, back to Roman times.

LinkedIn is multidimensional. It enables you deeply to explore who people are, what they've accomplished, and what they care about. As my friend Bob Donnell, says: "You are more than your business card."

While the first step is to click so as to connect, true connections involve patterns regarding with whom they are connected, their interests, groups, who they follow and by whom they are endorsed. A new connection for you, opens a potential kaleidoscope of connections.

I am a book lover, or more precisely, a lover of great authors. While recently perusing my library shelves, I became aware of how many authors had influenced other authors, most of whom, had also influenced me.

One title, a twenty-year old international bestseller "You Were Born Rich" was a book in which I had immersed myself, mainly because it's author, Bob Proctor, had studied from greats like Wallace D. Wattles (*The Science of Getting Rich*) and Napoleon Hill (*Think and Grow Rich*). Hill's landmark classic was first published in 1937, but remains a best seller with over 10 million copies sold.

Which by the way is a 78-year-old book that is still one of the top best sellers along with JK Rowling. So if you read *Harry Potter* and haven't read *Think and Grow Rich* you'll discover a different kind of magic.

When Bob Proctor is introduced, you hear a litany of accolades... international speaker, New York Times Best Seller, 6 million followers. But who is Bob Proctor? I discovered that he is truly a unique member of 'HumanKind". I met Bob Proctor at his mastermind event in Las Vegas, 20 years ago. The total number of people in the event were probably less than one-hundred. I don't remember everyone who was there, but what was very cool or coincidental, was that at least ten participants were in the 2006 film *The Secret*.

Give whatever you are doing and whoever you are with the gift of your attention.
--Jim Rohn

The interesting part is I didn't even realize through the years, how many of them I was connected with on LinkedIn. It was a real eye-opener for me, to suddenly be cognizant of how many connections I had that had languished through inattention. It was a big lesson for me.

Reflect for yourself, just a moment. How frequently in your life did you meet someone, got busy and didn't dive deeper or stay in touch? Take a real look at the people you connect with on LinkedIn and ask yourself, should I slow down, and examine what I really have enough here? If there truly are no coincidences, that each of your connections is there for a reason. Are you leveraging them?

Consider adding him to your influencer list.

Trust Your Intuition

Everything that happens in life happens for a reason. Every person you meet is a person you were supposed to meet. Some of those people will become close relationships, others you will introduce to someone you know, and others you will forge business relationships with. All of them, everyone you meet, know, and come in contact with, can become part of your LinkedIn network. Use your intuition and be creative when searching for connections. Some connections will jump right out. Others you will have to work to find.

When I chased after money, I never had enough. When I got my life on purpose and focused on giving of myself and everything that arrived into my life, then I was prosperous.
--Wayne Dyer

Connecting on LinkedIn is similar to going to a networking event and collecting business cards. When you approach a stranger, you need to connect with them before they will give you their card. I forget the psychology behind this, but usually you meet somebody, you look in your partner's right eye, which is the eye on your left. This intuitive reaction helps build rapport with the person you have just met. If you don't connect, you won't get the card and you definitely won't get anywhere when you follow up to talk to them later. It's about the relationship, finding a connection between the two of you. This is where your Sixth Sense needs to be sharp. What do you have in common with the person you want to connect with? My connection with Deepak was creativity. Look at the person or their profile and read between the lines. Did you come from the same state? Do you have similar hobbies? Using your intuition, find the piece of them that will best connect with a piece of you.

Once connected, you need to develop relationships with people. Relationships have to be managed and built over a period of time. Find a common bond or thread between you and build on that. It can be something silly, such as both of you love Lucy Ricardo and can sing the theme song to *Grease*. Even this small fact can start your relationship building.

Personal relationships are the fertile soil from which all advancement, all success, all achievement in real life grows.
--Ben Stein

For example, you might have a best friend you met at your last job who you haven't seen in two years. You've been building this relationship for years. If this friend were to call you in the middle of the night, say he was stranded at the airport with no way to get home, and ask you to come get him, you would probably go and pick him up. That is how deep you want your relationships to be. Relationships need to be based on quality, feeling, and trust. Once built on a strong foundation, those relationships will help build your chances of getting the job you want.

There is no such thing as a self-made man. You will reach your goals only with the help of others.
--George Shinn

You need to build 100 of these strong relationships. When you take time to build relationships in a strong manner, you will find all the connections you ever need. Maslow's law of building relationships with people states that you need a few basic things: air, water, food, sex, shelter, and significance. Everyone needs to feel significant in their lives. Connecting with people and giving them significance in your life allows you to expand your relationships.

ONE AND ONLY YOU

Every single blade of grass,
And every flake of snow –
Is just a wee bit different . .
There's no two alike, you know.

From something small, like grains of sand,
To each gigantic star
All were made with THIS in mind:
To be just what they are!

How foolish then, to imitate –
How useless to pretend!
Since each of us comes from a MIND
Whose ideas never end.

There'll only be just ONE of ME
To show what I can do –
And you should likewise feel very proud,
There's only ONE of YOU.

That is where it all starts
With you, a wonderful unlimited human being.

James T. Moore

Making Connections Anywhere

I recently gave a keynote speech at a local church. When the event was over, several people approached me to tell me the speech inspired them. They had no idea you could develop a human connection using LinkedIn. One individual made me stop and think. This individual had been in transition for a while and all she said was, "You gave me hope." She gets it. My passion for LinkedIn is based on the connections you make, which might give you the answers you've been searching for, gain you an interview, or give you hope on a day you need it. You never know when the very next connection you make might open the door.

Who should I invite?

Have you ever heard the term "fishbowl"? And no, I don't mean the bowl that your goldfish swim around in! Everyone has a fishbowl. Your fishbowl is your network of 10 to 100 friends and family members who like you, respect you, and support you.

LinkedIn helps you search your email

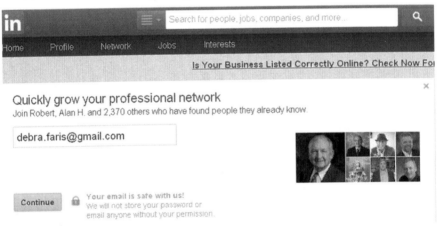

As you build your LinkedIn connections, make sure you build connections to your fishbowl, your 10 to 100 incredibly awesome people. One of the ways to do this is to find people they need to connect with. When you find such a connection, send it to them. They will open it and say, "Oh thank you!" It takes less than five seconds. It also takes less than five seconds to let your connections know you were thinking about them.

On each of your connections' profiles, next to the "Send a Message" button, you will find a bucket filled with actions you can take. One of them is "Share your Profile." If you find information on someone's profile that's beneficial to one of your connections, click the share button to send the profile to them. You can also use the button to follow up on someone you are not connected with yet but who you might want to connect with. These little bookmarks can make quite a difference for you.

You never get a second chance to make a first impression.
--Will Rogers

Pieces to the Puzzle: Memory Jogger

For me a memory jogger is like pieces to a puzzle. We all have different ways to put a puzzle together. Most people turn all the pieces over and sometimes section them by color. Other people like to use the box as a guide and work from the outside in. When putting your list together, the memory jogger can help you find people that you know but that you wouldn't immediately consider for inclusion.

The Memory Jogger		
People in your Community		
Tax Person	Fireman	Church
Policeman	Insurance Agent	Dentist
Car Dealer	School Teacher	Dry Cleaner
Hair Dresser	Mechanic	Plumber
Babysitter/Daycare	Chiropractor	Gardener
Pediatrician/Doctor		
Sports		
Golf	Bowling	Water Sports
Hunting	Football	Tennis

Baseball/Softball	Basketball	
Hobbies		
Cooking	Book Club	Music
Hiking	Traveling	
Life Events		
Weddings	Birthdays	
Employment		
Summer Jobs	Internships	
Clubs and Groups		
Corporate Alliances	Tennis club	Fraternity
Academic Decathlon	Sorority	
Multi-Cultural Student Leaders	Honors Programs	Leadership
Best Buddies		
School Acquaintances		
Elementary	Junior High	High School
College	Yearbook	

Should I accept anyone?

How many connections do I need? In a way, yes, there is a magic number. And the magic number is 500. It's like a bad haircut. You don't want people to think you don't have enough. Your results on LinkedIn will only be as good as the quality and variety of the connections you develop. You might get more results with 200 very close connections that resonate with you than with 2,000 connections that are just names.

You can have anything you want — if you want it badly enough. You can be anything you want to be, have anything you desire, accomplish

anything you set out to accomplish — if you will hold to that desire with singleness of purpose.
--Robert Collier

"Should I accept anyone who wants to connect?" The answer is simple. Think of accepting connections as like going to a party. You will find people you already know and are connected to. Then you'll meet people who form an instant connection with you. These are the people you know you like from the moment you start talking to them. Then you have the people that you don't connect with, don't like, and don't want to continue talking to. Your LinkedIn connections work the same way. Use your intuition to know whether or not this is someone that you want to have in your circle. If someone doesn't seem right for you and your career path, don't accept the invitation. If you like the person and want to get to know more about them and what they do, connect with them and begin the conversation.

Everyone has a purpose in life … a unique gift of special talent to give others. And when we blend this unique talent with service to others, we experience the ecstasy and exultation of our own spirit, which is the ultimate goal of all goals.
--Deepak Chopra

For some of you, accepting everyone will be fun and exciting as you build a huge network to draw on when the time comes. For others, your network may be more limited but more intimate, allowing in only those you're comfortable with and have built great relationships with. Both scenarios are effective. They work in different ways for different people.

One key question to ask is, "How much variety is there in my connections?" If you are self-employed, you might look for self-employed connections and pay attention to only the similarities between you and them. The smart person says, "I don't see the similarities between us, I see the differences." This is important because those differences mean that they have many connections you don't have. One of their connections might be a former CEO who could help with your job search.

It is in your moments of decision that your destiny is shaped.
--Tony Robbins

Our first inclination is to look for those like us. Often as human beings, we stay inside our own circles and gravitate towards people who are similar to us. However, a richer and more satisfying experience is possible if we include our polar opposites in our circle. Think outside the box and connect with people whom you can help or can help you. If you want to show off your musical talents, connect with bands, orchestras, the entertainment industry, schools, anything you can think of where music is important. Think outside the box and your possibilities will be endless.

When you connect with a person, always allow them to see all of your contacts, because that creates a measure of trust with the people you connect with. It's silly to hide your contacts, because that means you don't want to play the game. If you share your contacts and they're already in your fishbowl, your new connection may reciprocate, and you may find people that will fit into your fishbowl among their contacts.

Here are This Chapter's Business Consultant Influencers

As you read these profiles, look for possible referrals for your needs.

Is there something in their story you connect with?
Could you gain a new idea or insight for your business or career?
Who do you know or who do they know that can help both of you?
If you needed help or wanted to buy a product, what would it be?
How do you follow up when you meet someone?
When people view your profile, how do you want them to feel?
Do your tribes line up so you could be Power Partners?
What are your favorite questions to ask in an introductory call?

Todd Roberts

**Vice President, Group Benefits/
Coastal Financial Partners Group/**

Challenges are what make life interesting; overcoming them is what makes life meaningful. ~ Joshua J. Marine

I grew up in the entertainment business and my father started taking me to meetings at the age of two. My dad made 11 motion pictures as a Film Producer, was a Personal Manager to two dozen major names in the entertainment industry. He was humble and truthful to everyone he worked with. His ability to say the truth all the time, shaped how I handle my interactions with clients every day.

Today, I'm the Vice President of Group Benefits for Coastal Financial Partners Group. I'm known as a straight shooter, who always tells my clients the truth. Our team specializes in helping clients protect their wealth from higher taxes and uncertain times. I accrued over 30 years of experience in the financial services industry and am known as a professional who is committed to help people reach their financial and estate goals.

▶ GET LIFE INSURANCE.

▶ GET LONG TERM CARE INSURANCE, DISABILITY INCOME INSURANCE, FIXED ANNUITIES and QUALIFIED and NONQUALIFIED RETIREMENT PLANS

▶ PROTECT YOUR WEALTH

Specialties: Create Wealth, Accumulate Wealth, Protect Wealth, Life Insurance, Long Term Care Insurance, Disability Income Insurance, Fixed Annuities, Qualified and Nonqualified Retirement Plans, Employee Benefits including Group Medical, Business continuation & Estate Planning Services, Professional Policy Analysis and Review, Advanced Underwriting for Difficult Cases

What three books do you feel are a must that you highly recommend others to read? Iron John by Robert Bly. The ancient Hebrew legend of how to become a man and what it is to be a man. When Hollywood Had A King by Connie Bruck. The biography of Lew Wasserman, the man who built Universal into the mega media giant that it is. Heartland by Mort Sahl. A very prolific look at America.

What movie touched you by its meaning or inspired you? Casablanca, for its selflessness and self-sacrifice.

Who in your childhood was a major influence that helped shape your life? My parents, Lynne and Bobby Roberts. They gave me a strong work ethic, a sense of belonging, and taught me to be kind, humble, and grateful.

What will you do differently this year from last year or what do you want more of? 2018 will be a year where I have a plan that is truly mapped out. I plan to consolidate every business card/phone number I have been given over the years into a master email list, which I will utilize to market myself. I also plan to connect with every existing client.

What discipline could someone learn from you? My positive attitude and never giving up. My willingness to help and be of service.

When "winning someone over" do you think facts or emotions carry the day? This completely depends on who I am dealing with. I have to determine which of the four quadrants (controller/driver, analytical, emotional, promoter) the individual most likely fits into, and from there make that decision.

If there were one problem in the world you could solve, what would it be? My ultimate goal would be world peace. The question is whether or not world peace would come about on its own, or without first ending world hunger. People are more likely to listen to you with a full belly.

Todd's Favorite Characteristics
Connected, Strategic, Disciplined, Charismatic, Integrity, Optimistic, Service-Minded

Todd Roberts aka "Straight Shooter"
"We assist our Clients in the Creation and Preservation of Wealth in both their Business Endeavors and Personal Lives."
♛ Life Insurance ♕ Create Wealth ♛ Accumulate Wealth ♕ Protect Wealth
♟ Todd@CoastalFPG.com ♝ 310-299-8500 Ext 626 ♛
www.coastalfinancialpartnersgroup.com/ ✓

Pamela Gregory

Forgiveness Therapist, Speaker and Workshop Leader

"If love is all that matters in the end, shouldn't it be all that matters now."
~ Pamela Gregory

When I was 11 years old, tragedy struck. My idyllic world was turned upside down when my oldest brother, who I loved and adored, died of a major stroke in the brain at 21. I built a wall around my heart to protect myself. Many years later I realized the rock-solid wall wasn't protecting me, but it was robbing me of the love that makes life worth living. I learned how to love myself and others, and decided that I wanted to spend the rest of my life helping others set themselves free from their wounds.

Today my work and primary interest is geared toward helping my clients achieve and maintain "emotional fitness." I began my wellness career in the health and fitness industry over 30 years ago, and it involved into emotional fitness with a heavy emphasis on teaching the Science of Forgiveness. To this end, we conduct Workshops, provide Teaching Materials and offer Group and Private sessions to assist in restoring peace within Individual Hearts, Families, and Communities.

▶ Assisting Cancer Patients in Healing 'Dis-ease' of Body, Mind and Spirit in and outside of a clinical setting.

▶ Professionals with a variety of illnesses have had symptoms lessen, and even disappear when they learned to forgive.

▶ Family Forgiveness to assist clients in resolving their personal issues that are impacting their professional career.

Specialties: Healing Power of Forgiveness, Family Forgiveness, Consciousness, Frequency Medicine, Healing, Forgiveness, Resolution, Cancer Patients, Group & Private Lessons

What are your two favorite books you feel are a must that you highly recommend others to read? *The Four Agreements* by Don Miguel Ruiz. Honoring these four agreements helps keep one aligned with our highest self. *The Biology of Belief* by Bruce Lipton, PhD – He teaches we are not a victim of our heredity as we've been taught he gives us our power back. By changing our thoughts, we really do change our biology.

What does love mean to you? Love means to see oneself and others as our divine selves, who we were before our soul had a face. Love means to be free of judgments, to live and let live. Being free of judgment does not mean we lack discernment. Love means inclusion of all, regardless of how we differ.

Can forgiveness help us heal? Yes it can. When we harbor grievances, such as anger, grief, and guilt, it affects us at a cellular level until it is forgiven. Forgiveness heals when we see the transgression through the eyes of love and truth vs the story we created about the person or event. When we change what we made the event mean, negativity leaves and we heal in body, mind and spirit.

If you could start a movement, what would it be? My movement would be called LOVE7BILLION™. Imagine if 7 billion humans could all love and respect each other. Love is what we are here to Do and Be. Love Heals, Love Unites. Aligning with the frequency of LOVE will make a greater impact on the world than anything else.

In helping others, is it better to teach them, give them, or show them? I believe teaching others is the best way to help someone for once they have the tools, they can apply it to their life as often as needed. They can then share what they learned with others, creating a ripple of helping self and others.

What is one topic you really enjoy discussing with your contemporaries? I love talking about levels of consciousness and how they effect our lives, individually and collectively. When we consider that every thought creates a frequency, which creates matter, which creates our physical world, we grasp not only how powerful we are, but the level of responsibility we have to choose our thoughts consciously. No thing is created without thought.

Pamela's Favorite Characteristics
Compassionate, Passionate, Trustworthy, Genuineness, Sincere, Integrity, Loving, Kind

Pamela Gregory **aka** "The Forgiveness Queen"
"How Do You Mend a Broken Heart?. Pain and Heartbreak Can be Mended"
♛ International Forgiveness Consultant & Healing Coach ♚ Speaker ♛
Workshop Leader ♚ Radio Show Host ♚ EFT Practitioner
♟ pamela@pamelagregory.com ♟ 954-295-1417 ♛
www.pamelagregory.com √

Cecile Licauco DDS

Dentist & Entrepreneur

"In every day, there are 1,440 minutes. That means we have 1,440 daily opportunities to make a positive impact." ~ Les Brown

I became a dentist because as a child I was afraid of them even if they were excellent. Unfortunately, I had bad teeth which exacerbated the problem. I decided to go to dental school to become the gentle dentist that could relate to my patients that I never had when I was young.

Today I run my own practice, Orange Park Smile Studio. Our purpose is to help our patients young and old achieve the highest levels of dental health and well-being with a sense of caring, comfort, kindness & personal service.

Many of our patients are professionals who may not feel comfortable about their smile. After having braces and implants one of our clients, a professional speaker who was insecure about her smile, grew her business exponentially because she was got a major boost in her self confidence

▶ Family Dentistry, Braces

▶ Professionals. If you're feeling somewhat self-conscious about your teeth, or just want to improve your smile, cosmetic dental treatments may be the answer to a more beautiful, confident smile.

▶ Implants. Will Change the way you Eat, and you Feel about Yourself

While we continue to grow, we are never too busy to help serve your family, friends, neighbors and business associates. It's an honor and a pleasure to help them achieve the smile of their dreams.

SPECIALTIES:

Family Dentistry, Orthodontics (Traditional, Invisalign), Cosmetic, Sports, Implants, Laser Dentistry, Digital X-rays, Gum Lift

Who in your childhood was a major influence that helped shape your life? My father was a major influence growing up. He loved unconditionally, worked very hard and always had a positive attitude despite all the trials & tribulations in business and in life.

What will you do differently this year from last year or what do you want more of? I will focus more intently on being a better person than I've ever been in business and in life.

Who now is a Mentor, Coach or Strategist that is on your advisory council? Les Brown, John-Leslie Brown & Dr. Carol Soloway. I believe in them and they believe in me.

If you could be anyone for a day, who would it be and what experience can you envision? Oprah Winfrey. I could envision a strong woman who goes after what she wants and still has the humility to learn from others.

What discipline could someone learn from you? The discipline of doing what one fears the most, being persistent & staying calm through storms.

What subject or argument most stirs your emotions, why? The idea that people are so different. I believe that although there are cultural differences, people desire the same things...happiness, love, honesty & the desire to do good for others

Cecile's Favorite Characteristics
Committed, Gentle in the Mouth, Upbeat, Passionate, Professional, Recovering Perfectionist, Compassionate

Dr. Cecile Licauco aka *"The Gentle Lady Dentist"*
"Reach out now. We'll give you a reason to smile."
Les Brown's business strategist & John-Leslie Brown's chief of staff
♛ Leadership Speaker ♛ Motivational Speaker ♛ Corporate Facilitator
♛ Executive Coach
♜ ♞ 714-984-2050 ♛ smileremedynow@gmail.com ♛
www.smileremedynow.com ✓

Learning 2.0

The more I search, the more I find,

The more I find, the more I read,

The more I read, the more I think,

The more I think, the more I learn,

The more I learn, the more I do,

The more I do, the more I create,

The more I create, the more I share,

The more I share, the more I collaborate,

The more I collaborate, the more I connect,

The more I connect, the more I learn,
the more I KNOW

And the more Intelligent

I GROW!

Cheryl Capozzoli

Chapter 4
To Engage or Not to Engage

Your smile will give you a positive countenance that will make people feel comfortable around you.

--Les Brown

Les Brown

Learn Speaking Secrets from 1 of TOP 5 world speakers. For Speaker's Training go now to our website LesBrownSpeaking,com

Greater Los Angeles Area | Professional Training & Coaching

| Current | KFWB, Les Brown Enterprises, LLC, www.LesBrownSpeaking.com |
| Previous | www.lesbrown.com |

Send a message ▼

500+
connections

My Influencers: Les Brown

Back in the early 80's, I would go every motivational speaking event and I got hooked on Zig Ziglar and Les Brown. All I had to hear was this charismatic voice "Good Morning, I'm Les Brown, Mamie Brown's Baby Boy" This big teddy bear would share how we all had greatness in us and encourage us to "Live Our Dream".

I just love coincidences. A little over a year ago, I got invited by some friends to have dinner with Les and a dozen of his friends. I felt like I won the lottery! A year later, I am part of Bob Donnell's *Next Level by Association*. Bob invites a friend as a special guest to his monthly dinners, and as I was catching up with some friends...I heard a laugh and I stopped in my tracks. In my head, "I said I know that laugh, I know that laugh…". I turned around and I thought I was in a time machine thrown back 25 years. There he was a spitting image of his father Les Brown. Holy-Moly it is Les Brown's Baby Boy John-Leslie Brown. The night just got better and better. How did I get so lucky to be blessed to hear the echo of his father? Thank you, Mamie Brown, for being an influencer of these beautiful men that have consistently made a big difference in people's lives spanning decades.

Consider adding him to your influencer list.

Who Viewed You?

Do you remember the story of *The Tortoise and the Hare*? What about the phrase, "Slow and steady wins the race?" In both of these fables from childhood, the moral is that being persistent and taking things one step at a time will get you the results you desire. One of the 12 traits of over-achievers outlined in one of the most famous books in personal development history, *Think & Grow Rich* by Napoleon Hill, is to take small steps every day to accomplish your goals. The Tortoise who schedules five minutes every day will progress farther than the Hare who creates a burst of energy every few weeks. If you spend five minutes a day on LinkedIn, you will be like the early bird that gets the worm.

Shoot for the moon and if you miss you will still be among the stars.
--Les Brown

One of the most important tasks you can do in your five minutes a day is look at the five most recent persons to view your LinkedIn profile. This is a great advantage LinkedIn provides since no other websites give you that information. With this information, you can now view that person's profile and learn more about them.

First, look at how you are connected to them (if at all). Note the common traits, desires, and goals you share. Then look at what you do not share with this person. If you share nothing, there is always potential for you to be their polar opposite.

This person viewed you for a reason and that starts to forge a connection between the two of you, again for a reason. Even if you have nothing in common with this person, you should either send them an invite to connect or share their profile with someone you think would connect well with them. Helping other people today will make their tomorrow better and they will remember you in your future.

Shared Connections Are Gold

Earlier, I showed you how to identify the 10 to 100 most important people in your life. These are the people you invite to your wedding or who will attend your funeral, the people who are most visible in your life and in many cases the most likely to help you in time of need.

Although you want to develop and cultivate all of your LinkedIn connections, these 100 people may hold the key to your future. You need to build a connection with them at an emotional level, both one-on-one and in a group. People don't care about how much you know until they know how much you care. Spend time and energy fostering a strong relationship with these individuals. From there, you can build more distant connections and share your most important connections with people who would appreciate knowing them. It's important to share your connections with others and continue to foster strong relationships.

Lee Shares 164

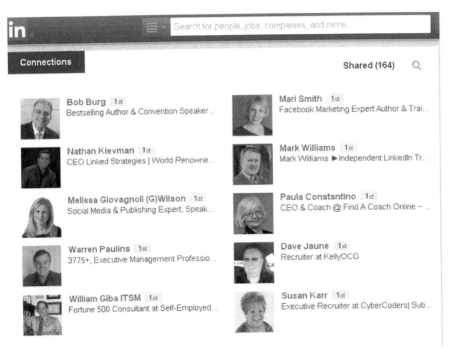

Sharing your connections is simple. When you find a connection that you know someone else can use, move your cursor to the right of the "Send InMail" button and right click; a drop-down menu will appear, select "Share" and follow the steps. The person you are sending the connection to will get a LinkedIn "In Mail" with their profile attached. This is your opportunity to help those that are helping you.

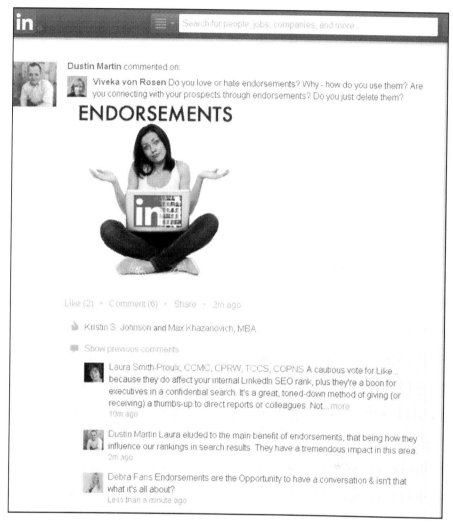

To Endorse or Not to Endorse

In the beginning, when LinkedIn brought endorsements to their platform, I had numerous calls from people confused as to what it was and why someone they didn't know was endorsing them. Some people find change difficult because they don't understand it. However, people who were used to Facebook were comfortable with the new addition to LinkedIn since it gave them an opportunity to have an online conversation by acknowledging something they liked about another profile, which they couldn't do anywhere else. I took a deep breath and realized that people's frustration came from a lack of understanding about the value of this new feature. One client I was working with was very confused. I explained to him that it was actually a compliment. The first question I asked was, "Did you look at your profile and search for the person's name and are they a first level connection?" Out of embarrassment but honesty, he acknowledged they were first connections.

I said, "Do you remember this person?"

Engage By Endorsements

After a moment's pause, he scanned the profile and said, "Oh, I remember him."

I asked, "Is there something in his profile that you like that could get the conversation rolling?"

After looking at the profile, he found three things he liked and found a way to do business with the other party. When the ball bounces to your side of the court, it's your turn to give back. You can endorse a skill on his profile or take it one step deeper and send him a LinkedIn message. Within the week, he sent me a thank you back and said he was meeting his new LinkedIn friend in person.

Social media is changing the way we communicate and the way we are perceived, both positively and negatively. Every time you post a photo, or update your status, you are contributing to your own digital footprint and personal brand.
--Amy Jo Martin

When you notice a person who has over 99 endorsements, find the skill that's most endorsed on that profile that most resonates with you. Let's say its creativity. When you move your cursor to the right on the line where the photos are, it will show you everyone who has endorsed that person. It's fun to see who your first connections are but another opportunity to grow your LinkedIn connections is to look at level people who you can network with or who can help you build you path to an exciting job.

Positioning and Aligning

When you build your LinkedIn profile, it's important to use your character words with your skills in an alignment that is in harmony with your purpose and intentions. If you want to be promoted to CFO and your profile shows that in previous positions you worked in the sales department but not in accounting, you will confuse those looking at your profile. However, if you worked for the accounting department, even in a support position, you need to make that experience clear.

You position yourself when you find other LinkedIn members who do what you do or what you want to do and connect with them. This begins to build your well. When you're connected to someone who does what you want, other people will see you and you can move into their circles and connect with them.

Here are This Chapter's
Business Consultant Influencers

As you read these profiles, look for possible referrals for your needs.

Is there something in their story you connect with?

Could you gain a new idea or insight for your business or career?

Who do you know or who do they know that can help both of you?

If you needed help or wanted to buy a product, what would it be?

How do you follow up when you meet someone?

When people view your profile, how do you want them to feel?

Do your tribes line up so you could be Power Partners?

What are your favorite questions to ask in an introductory call?

Ana Weber

~Business Rainmaker~
Money Flow & The DOXA Method

"We will always tend to fulfill our own expectations of ourselves."
~ Brian Tracy

Who would have believed it? Ana made it! She was born in Romania during the communist regime and raised by a single mother, totally sheltered, insecure and a complete introvert. At the age of 11 she and her mother immigrated to Israel, pursuing a new life, more opportunities and freedom.

Today Ana is the founder of the DOXA METHOD, transport your fears into success. She empowers people and leaders from all over the world to conquer challenges and look at stress as opportunities. THE DOXA METHOD is a success formula Ana introduced and implemented at the various organizations she held leadership positions such as CEO, CFO, VP of Sales in the various industries: clothing manufacturing, medical devices, Hospitality, automotive manufacturing, architectural signs (Smithsonian Institute) Porsche Race Car Division.

Since 2005 she has published 17 nonfiction books on personal improvement, as well as a novel and a poetry collection. *The Money Flow*, published in 2013 is an Amazon #1 bestseller.

Design your Life, **O**pen Doors, Become E**X**traordinary, Take **A**ction

► Personal Coaching

► Online Coaching

► Speaking

SPECIALTIES: Personal Coaching, Online Coaching, Money Management, Relationship Management, Time Management, Energy Management, Leadership Development, Speaking

Who in your childhood was a major influence that helped shape your life? My Mother... She is a Hero, She is a Holocaust Survivor she beat hunger coming back at 59 pounds. She never gives up on anything, she beat cancer, the strongest character I've ever known, she's dynamic & energetic

If you could be anyone for a day, who would it be and what experience can you envision? Mother Teresa

What will you do differently this year from last year or what do you want more of? I want to increase my marketing, visibility & & exposure for more sales & commissions

What discipline could someone learn from you? Time Management, I don't get overwhelmed, I accomplish everything I set out to 1 step or project at a time

If you could have any superpower (or be any superhero), what/who would it be and why? Oprah Winfrey, Her superpower is people listen and believe her goodness

When "winning someone over" do you think facts or emotions carry the day? Emotions, first and latter you blend it with logic

Ana's Favorite Characteristics
Open Minded, Strategist, MindFulness, Money Flow, End in Mind Thinking

Ana Weber, Ph.D, MBA, CPC aka "The DOXA Coach"
"Realize **D**esire, Create **O**pportunity, Become E**X**ceptional, **A**chieve Goals"
♛ Business, Professional & Personal Lifestyle Leadership Coach ♛ The Doxa Method ♛ ♛ ♟ ana@anaweberdoxa.com ☎ 949-422-1830 ♛
www.anaweberdoxa.com ✓

Eddie Martin

**Training Expert /
Client Relationship Specialist /
Networking Advocate / Sales Enthusiast /
Social Media Marketing / Blogger /
Branding / Live Video Content Creator**

"Only those who will risk going too far can possibly find out how far one can go." T.S. Eliot

When I was 16 years old, my parents divorced, and I was told that if was to be, it was up to me. It only took another 10 years to realize that was the truth. I've spent the last several years developing myself, my skills and a student mindset. Raising my 3 children has been the greatest and most rewarding challenge in my life to date.

Today I meet with the world's leading subject matter experts and show them how to virtualize their intellectual property and leverage their brand by replicating themselves. This frees them up to spend time doing what they love most.

▶ World changing subject matter experts seeking a business model that will optimize and scale their impact on their specific market.

▶ Business owners that understand that the greatest investment that they can have in their business is effectively training and educating their staff.

▶ Professionals looking to build key relationships with a network of like-minded individuals.

SPECIALTIES: Education / Training / Sales / Networking / Recurring Revenue / Strategic Planning / Interactivity / elearning / Marketing / Social Media / influence / Speakers / Trainers / Coaches / Fortune 500 / Small Business / Medium Business / MLM / Network Marketing / Associations /

What three books do you feel are a must that you highly recommend others to read? *The Richest Man in Babylon* by George S. Clason will teach you the principles of money. *Think and Grow Rich* by Napoleon Hill will teach you the power of your mind and intentions. *Extreme Ownership* by Jocko Willink & Leif Babin will teach you the power of commitment and responsibility.

What movie touched you by its meaning or inspired you? Forest Gump was an inspiration to me because it was an against all odds story. You learn that no matter who you are or what challenges life throws at you, if you are committed to success, you will be successful.

Who in your childhood was a major influence that helped shape your life? My grandfather taught me that you can have anything that you want if you refuse to take "no" for an answer. He did not tell me this, he showed me in his actions.

Who now is a Mentor, Coach or Strategist that is on your advisory council? Brad Lea, Tammy Kling, Vick Tipnes and Tony Capullo

What discipline could someone learn from you, Persistence and determination are the two disciplines that someone could learn from me.

When "winning someone over" do you think facts or emotions carry the day? People justify emotions with logic. They are both necessary to effectively "win someone over."

In helping others, is it better to teach them, give them, or show them? This depends on who and what you are teaching. Sometimes it is best to lead the horse to the water and other times it is necessary to dunk them in it. While other times you need to show them that it is safe to drink it.

Eddie's Favorite Characteristics
Father, Friend, Leader, Student, Mentee, Creative, Networker

Eddie Martin aka "Catapult Your Vision through Artificial Intelligence"
▶ EddieMartin@lightspeedvt.com ◀
▶ 916-430-7559 ◀ ▶ http://LightSpeedVT.com

"Develop Trust and Rapport and you make a friend. Deliver a Script and you make a Sale!" --John Kurth

My family members were highly educated and very articulate in expressing their views. When I was young, I discovered the power of language to influence and get results. My love of language continued in college and in graduate school where I studied Mandarin Chinese and earned an international MBA. I worked and lived in Hong Kong, Mainland China, and in Taiwan. Upon my return, I founded my company Syntactics Sales Scripting®.

Today it is my mission to help other sales executives, entrepreneurs, and sales people to create winning Sales Scripts that empower them to close sale-after-sale! I help make your sales communications comprehensive, substantial, and precise.

▶A client attended a tradeshow and only received 3 qualified leads. After working with me to develop their Tradeshow Scripts, they received 45 qualified leads at their next tradeshow!

▶A retirement community's sales force was quite young and was working with clients who were 65 years and older. The sales people didn't know how to craft their message to match their target market. I crafted their Sales Scripts and Trained the sales team who are consistently winning more customers with their Sales Scripts.

▶A professional speaker was delivering a 2-day workshop and not making many sales. I helped craft 16 hours of content. The client now closes 25-60% of the room and has $100,000 dollar events.

Specialties: Sales Script Trainer/Sales Script Coach/Keynote Speaker/ Workshop Leader/ Leadership/ Sales / Marketing/ Business Automation

What 3 books do you feel are a must that you highly recommend others to read? *The E-Myth Revisited* by Michael Gerber explains how to take a systems approach to your business and your life. *Sales Management* by Robert J. Calvin describes how to develop a top-producing sales force which is essential to growing a successful business. And my own book, *What Are Your Words Wearing?* explains the power of Sales Scripting and how it can transform your business.

Who in your childhood was a major influence that helped shape your life? My high school History teacher opened the world of history and biography as a source of inspiration.

What will you do differently this year from last year? I will systematize my business even more. Developing more systems for my business is working "on" my business and not just "in" my business.

What discipline could someone learn from you? People can learn how to use their language with precision to get more of what they want out of life.

When "winning someone over" do you think facts or emotions carry the day? Selling and Persuasion is 80% psychology. That's why I take a Neuro-Linguistic Programming (NLP) approach to developing Sales Scripts. The psychology behind the communication is what makes it work.

In helping others, is it better to teach them, give them, or show them? Show them first. Experts have the experience to show their clients what to do so they get results right away. The next step is to teach them so clients can do it themselves.

If there were one problem in the world you could solve, what would it be? People are texting and emailing so much that they are losing their ability to truly communicate. I would help people re-connect to the power of their spoken language to communicate effectively.

John's Favorite Characteristics
Authentic, Comprehensive, Compassionate, Substantial, Precise, Expressive, and Organized

John Kurth - Sales Script Coach "Develop High-Performing Scripts That Close Sales"
Author of *What Are Your Words Wearing? How to Make Your Sales Communications Comprehensive, Substantial, and Precise*
*Email: john@syntaxofsuccess.com * Tel: 714-688-6443 *
www.syntaxofsuccess.com
linked-in address: www.linkedin.com/in/johndkurth

One of the most powerful

networking practices

is to provide

immediate value

to a new connection.

This means the moment

you identify

a way to help someone,

take action.

Lewis Howes

Chapter 5
Networking to the Next Level

First, you have to be visible in the community. You have to get out there and connect with people. It's not called net-sitting or net-eating. It's called networking. You have to work at it.

-- **Ivan Misner**

Ivan Misner
Founder of BNI and Referral Institute
Austin, Texas | Marketing and Advertising

Current   BNI, BNI Foundation, Referral Institute
Education   USC

Send a message   Endorse ▾   **500+**
connections

My Influencers: Ivan Meisner

The day before my son passed away, he said, "Things happen for a reason." It came true for me when a friend convinced me to go to a networking meeting at the Long Beach convention center only to find it was happening the following week.

As I looked around, I saw a banner that said BNI. It's a great group, and the thought popped into my head, "Is the founder here?" Even thought it was a far-fetched coincidence, I asked the first person I saw, "By chance is Mr. Misner here?" The person said, "Yes, he is and he's standing three feet away."

To my delight I reached my hand out and said, "Hi, my name is Debra Faris It is such an honor to meet you." Now catch this. I knew BNI was a great networking group organized in 55 countries with 150,000 members to help people network, generating millions of referrals. Their LinkedIn group has over 36,000 members.

Dr. Misner is called the Father of Modern Networking. He has written 12 books, including his recent #1 bestseller, *Networking like a Pro*. He has been featured in the Wall Street Journal, the New York. Times, TV and radio shows including CNN, CNBC, and the BBC in London.

For those of you who like non-profits, he is founder of the BNI Misner Charitable Foundation and has been named Humanitarian of the Year.

Consider adding him to your influencer list.

Your Million Dollar Message

I never thought I needed a pitch when I met people. Then I attended an executive networking group that held a training class once a week. Part of the curriculum to train people who had lost their jobs (in transition) was how to create a pitch. Since I had been in the banking industry for 15 years and the banks were disintegrating, I figured I needed to check this class out. The curriculum taught students how to write a resume, have a mock interview, learn how to network, and to create a 30-second elevator Pitch. They taught that you need to know how to tell people in an instant in a clear and concise manner who you are and what you're looking for. It was a great way for me to sharpen my skills and acquire new ones.

When I stepped into the class, it all seemed so natural for me that they were surprised with my natural unconventional networking manner. They were so impressed that they asked me to be one of the trainers. Two weeks later I stepped into the trainer position and two weeks after that they made me a lead trainer. It was cool being a trainer because I was helping people and at the same time honing my own skills.

One day I worked with a man in his 50s who had been a CFO (Chief Financial Officer) for over 25 years. He had only two jobs in his entire career, was making over a quarter million a year, and had been with the same company for over a dozen years. At the end of one day, I told the class that the next day we would give our 30-

second pitch. As I handed him the assignment so he could prepare for the next day, he looked at me with a puzzled expression.

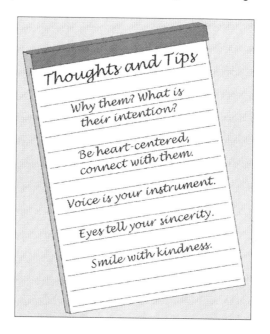

Thoughts and Tips

Why them? What is their intention?

Be heart-centered, connect with them.

Voice is your instrument.

Eyes tell your sincerity.

Smile with kindness.

He showed up the next day and took his seat among the 14 people in the class. I put an example of a 120-word pitch up on the screen. "You need to present this pitch in 30 seconds or less," I said. His face reflected the look of an individual clearly apprehensive about taking on this task, but also determination to give it all he had. He had been a leader all his life, and this C-level executive wanted people to see him as a prospect for any job his new-found peers might know about. I saw hesitation. When his turn came, he stood and started to introduce himself but got so caught up in trying to remember the words that he stuttered and turned 50 shades of red. Did I say that this man was about 6'4" and weighed at least 220 pounds? I'm 5'3" and a little thing next to this big guy.

When the rubber meets the road you just jump in with both feet. I wanted him to know I would be his wingman and together we could do this. I stood next to him. His eyes were filled with tears. It broke my heart to see such a prideful man feel like he was a failure.

I remembered a Tony Robbins seminar I had attended where I learned about pattern interruptions. This would be the perfect time for me to share this technique with the class and make it fun at the same time. I told them, "Let's do the Hokey Pokey and turn ourselves around." They humored me and did the exercise as I instructed them. I could see the confusion on my CFO's face.

When we finished, I said, "Now, tell everyone what industry you are most interested in and tell everyone one thing that you could do to help them."

The man, now much more at ease, told everyone that he would be happy to help any of the class members by introducing them to any of his LinkedIn contacts. He then added that it would be an honor to do so and that his name was John Smith. He ended his 30-second pitch with, "Thank you very much. It's nice to meet all of you." The class jumped to their feet and gave him a standing ovation. It made me feel like I had made a huge difference for him.

In this situation, the man had shifted from thinking with his head to feeling with his heart. He functioned from a place of laughter and compassion.

When teaching you to create your own pitch, trainers will tell you, "Stand in front of the mirror and go blah, blah, blah." An even better option is to talk to a doll or teddy bear or the cutest thing you ever saw. When we talk to ourselves in the mirror we were talking from our heads. When we talk to another object, we are talking from our hearts. You shift into your being, your conversations, your body, and your caring. You come from laughter and compassion. You shift and your pitch shifts with you.

That's what has to happen on your LinkedIn. When you shift from being all about me to being all about what they need, everything shifts for you.

You also need to shift your conversations from your body to being and caring. On your LinkedIn profile, shift from thinking about yourself and what you can get out of a connection to thinking about what you can do for the other person. You will forge real connections where you will find true benefits. If you aren't thinking about whom your audience is, they may be repelled by what you have to say. If you pay attention to them, you will tailor the conversation that honors who they are. That will get you connections that matter.

F.O.R.M.

A lot of people ask me, "How do I network? How do I know who, when, where and how?" It is easy to figure this out, because people are attracted to like-minded people who share a common taste in things such as clothing, hobbies and careers.

When you understand this, you can learn to network any time anywhere. I learned this process in a network marketing company and it is still used all over the world in many companies. You can use it every day whether you are sitting in a dentist's office or you are networking at a social event.

The "Who am I" who shows up is your integrity, your loyalty, your dependability, your creativity, all the human character traits that you bring to your networking.

The acronym for this process is F.O.R.M.

F is for where they are From. I also like to ask where they were born. I have found that many people have known their friends for many years but never knew whether these friends came from a place they had in common or had a place they always wanted to explore.

O is for your Occupation. Asking a new connection what industry they work in is important both for someone who is in transition or someone who already works for a company.

R is your Recreation. A lot of people like to talk about their hobbies and what they do on weekends.

M is your Message. Your message is how you can help potential employers when you are looking for a job.

From: You ask your new connection two questions, "Where are you from?" and "Where were you born?" You wait for the answers, take two seconds to pause. After you give your connection the opportunity to share where they are from, reflect back to them where you were born and where you live. You may discover you have something in common.

Occupation: What do you do or what industry are you in? Remember, if your connection is in transition and the networking event is about job-hunting, stick to mentioning your industry and don't add who you work for. Reflect back to them the parts of your career that complement their past or present career.

Recreation: You may meet someone at a social gathering or fun event. It is easy to start a conversation about the hobbies, sports, or other fun things. Reflect commonalities between you, which will build a bond as each of you discovers more about the other.

Message: Now that you have established rapport, you can share that you are on LinkedIn and would be happy to help them with some of your connections. Ask yourself, "What is the one key thing that I could ask if they need help with."

Qualify like a CEO

Let's say you have become a CFO who works in Los Angeles, but you commute 50 miles from Orange County and you would like to find a job closer to home in Orange County.

If you're not making mistakes, then you're not doing anything. I'm positive that a doer makes mistakes.
--John Wooden

One ideal way to make that happen is find a referring partner. First you go to LinkedIn and find a CFO that's in transition and ask him to visit you in Orange County. You sit down for breakfast or lunch with this partner and say, "You're a CFO and I'm a CFO and my wife would be very unhappy if we moved out of Orange County because our kids and our church are here. I know that you want to work in Los Angeles and I want to work in Orange County. How about sharing leads? I can give you leads I hear about in Los Angeles and you can share Orange County leads with me."

I have a dream that my four little children will one day live in a nation where they will not be judged by the color of their skin, but by the content of their character.
--Martin Luther King, Jr.

Remember that people are people and have needs that they have to take care of. If you eliminate the fear that you might take away another person's position, you now have as a partner a 100% invested person that has the same goal as you. Working together and networking in your respective areas, you can help each other be successful.

Networking Tips

1. Keep your body language open if you want to get to know someone. Hold your shoulders a little bit back. When you shake their hand, look them in the eye.

2. When you are at a networking event where you want to meet people, everybody has a comfort zone. If you sense you are too close based on the other person's reaction, step back. They are telling you that you are in their space. It's nothing to be offended over, just give them more space.

3. Networking is about getting out of your head and into your heart.

4. People need to feel comfortable with who you are and how you show up.

5. When you network, you have to change hats depending on your audience. You wouldn't talk in a business office like you would talk at a baseball game. You have to think from your audience's perspective.

6. When you smile, you show another of your human sides and people will feel comfortable with you.

7. Remember to keep your questions light. People don't like to feel that they are being interrogated.

8. Keep your conversations and your body in a caring posture. Come from laughter and compassion.

9. Sometimes we can give too much information about ourselves and then people make judgments.

10. When all else fails and you don't know who to talk to, look for the guy or gal who is standing alone and seems to be thinking, "Why am I here?" He knows why he's there. He just doesn't know how to approach other people. So be the hero and start conversations with F.O.R.M.

What is Left-Brain Right-Brain connecting?

I'm sure you've heard the terms "Left-Brained" and "Right-Brained" before, but have you ever considered the depth of the terms' meaning? A Left-Brained individual is a person who utilizes mostly the left side of their brain, making that individual more analytical, logical, and objective. A Right-Brained individual uses mostly the right side of their brain, which leads to a more subjective, thoughtful, and intuitive approach.

Left-Brain dominant individuals typically fill roles such as CFO (Chief Financial Officer) and COO (Chief Operating Officer) due to their analytical capabilities. Right-Brain dominant individuals typically fill roles such as CMO (Chief Marketing Officer), CNO (Chief Networking Officer) and CEO (Chief Executive Officer), although these people can fall into either category depending on whether they were appointed or founded the company.

When I work with C-level Left-Brained dominant individuals who love equations and analytics, I find that trying to get them to do anything creative or unorthodox makes them uncomfortable. When I work with the Right-Brained dominant individuals, who love creativity, they get lost in the massive amount of information analytics provides. It dawned on me that the perfect pairing was to match Left-Brained and Right-Brained persons, who will then complement each other perfectly and produce both the analysis and the creativity that successful companies and people require.

This concept also works when two opposite individuals work together on LinkedIn. The "Right-Brain" dominant person can create a more attractive profile while the "Left-Brained" dominant individual can create more detailed content and catch errors that are not obvious. When two people from opposite sides of the coin get together, they will produce a more balanced and robust LinkedIn profile. This pertains to writing a profile and also works amazingly well in person when connecting with another human being.

Character isn't something you were born with and can't change, like your fingerprints. It's something you weren't born with and must take responsibility for forming.
--Jim Rohn

A Left-Brained individual may stand in a corner and analyze the room. They might come from a place of judgment versus the place of observation the Right-Brained individual prefers. Each will communicate in different styles and operate in different styles. Yet when they work together, they complement each other and help each other by introducing new contacts they could not have discovered alone. This is a great way to network since the Left-Brained individual is good with detail and can be a great accountability partner for the Right-Brained individual. Each individual will open doors for the other, creating a perfectly balanced networking team.

Try this out by meeting at least three people who are your opposites the next time you go to a networking event. If you are an extrovert, look for someone who is more introverted. If you are creative, look for a good organizer. If you think you are introverted and not a networker, look for the friendliest person in the room and start a conversation. You will meet your exact opposite, the very person you need to meet, because when the two of you come together you never know what might happen.

The Deeper You Go, the Closer You Get to Gold

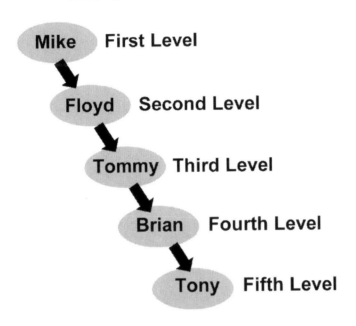

Mike — First Level

Floyd — Second Level

Tommy — Third Level

Brian — Fourth Level

Tony — Fifth Level

Go Deep in Your Connections

In the book *Think and Grow Rich*, Napoleon Hill tells the story of R. U. Darby, a Maryland businessman who discovered a rich vein of gold in the Colorado Mountains. They followed the vein until it gave out. Certain that no more gold existed, they quit and sold out to a junk dealer, who found a new vein of gold just three feet away from where Darby had stopped. The junk man made millions. So I want to share with you, many people give up when they are only three feet away!

In social media it is a common to hear people say, "Six Degrees to Kevin Bacon" phrase, because people realized that through this person they could ask someone do you know someone who knows Kevin Bacon and then they would continue to ask so on and so forth.

In theory, this means everyone in the world is connected to everyone else in the world by a chain of no more than six people. This was shown in the movie, *Six Degrees of Separation* with Kevin Bacon. With LinkedIn I have found people with three or four searches. The closer the alignment the closer you are to finding them.

With a few searches on LinkedIn, you can find almost anyone you want to connect with because LinkedIn can link you to 300 million of the billions of people on our planet.

Network Like Your Life Depends on It

When a recruiter or an influential individual meets they will mentally place you in one of four buckets: Yes. No. Maybe.!

The key to coming across as a potential partner, he says, is to use confidence and communication skills (both are skills that can be learned!) to stand out from the crowd and building *personal relationships* with influential individuals. The key includes having a range of diversity within your network.

For example, if you are Salesperson, it's important to develop relationships with individuals who are in other disciplines who have different values and perspectives, such as Accounting or Engineering. This diversity in networks is beneficial for a variety of reasons:

1. It enables you to be a connector who can bring two usually separate groups of people together.

2. It allows you to be more self-aware and open-minded by understanding a diversity of viewpoints

3. It exposes you to opportunities that you may not be aware of

"It's not always easy to build a relationship with a person who is different from you," Jaymin Patel says. "However, it's easier than you might think. Use my Three Word Intro, which goes like this: 'Hi, I'm Jaymin.'"

This approach works 99% of the time, he says. "When the other person does not respond it's ok. Just use the Three Word Intro on the next person! For best results, use it in an environment common to the individual you are speaking with."

Once Jaymin used the Three Word Intro on a plane. That stranger became one of the most impactful individuals in his career. "He connected me with an opportunity I wasn't aware of," he said. "I left my full-time job and became an author, speaker, and coach reaching thousands around the world."

He added, "When you know how to start a conversation with anyone, you can build diversity into your network by networking like a ROCKSTAR!"

Who are the top 10 most powerful connections you have? The people who can make things happen for you! Then ask yourself, what have I done for these people lately? Or, maybe a better question is, are these people you just call every once in a while to suck their blood.
--Jeffrey Gitomer

Relationship Currency

Relationship Currency is such an interesting topic. When he speaks about relationship bank accounts Steven Covey says "First seek to understand then to be understood." If you had an account that had $1,000 and all you did was take money out and never to make any deposits, it wouldn't be too long before it was empty. There used to be a saying save your pennies for a rainy day (now it would be dollars). However, there are some people who will ask again and again for things and we may feel like they never give anything in return. The same goes on in networking and on LinkedIn. People will ask for a recommendation and they have never even made another point of communication after the initial invite, not alone a phone call but they want you to recommend them? It's kind of confusing especially when you are new and you want to build someone relationships. So how do you build your own LinkedIn currency? Here are a few tips:

1. Looking through your new updates and when you see one of your new connections got a job, send them congratulations.

2. Someone has a new photo, tell them you noticed.

3. You see a new member in a group, go look at their profile and then send them a welcome to the group with a nice comment about their profile and send them a welcome with a nice comment

4. When you see a job that is in the industry of one of your top 20 send them the Link of forward them the job posting.

5. When you see a charity on one of your friend's profiles, ask them more about it.

Go confidently in the direction of your dreams. Live the life you have imagined.
--Henry David Thoreau

How to Win Friends and Influence People

Sometimes life comes full circle. One of the very first leadership training courses I took was Dale Carnegie. At the time I didn't know Mr. Carnegie had passed before I was born. The core values and principles he taught are timeless. Many years later in Vegas, I attended Author 101 heard Jill Lublin, author of the best seller *Networking Magic* speak.

Later that afternoon I bumped into her in the hall, had a nice chat, and exchanged cards, just enjoying our moment together and connecting. I thanked her for her words of wisdom.

Later I looked her up on LinkedIn and discovered she was a modern-day Dale Carnegie on how to be influential. She's been featured in the New York Times, Women's Day, Fortune, Small Business, Inc., and Entrepreneur Magazine, and on ABC, CBS, NBC TV and radio. When your values align with other great peoples values it creates a strong foundation for new relationships.

Here's one of Jill's tried and true philosophies:

*Without introductions, matches can't be made.

*Without matches, connections cannot be created.

*Without connections, bonds cannot form

*Without bonding, relationships cannot be built and

*Without reciprocal relationships, networks cannot last

*Continue to grow your friendships to the next level.

Here are This Chapter's Business Consultant Influencers

As you read these profiles, look for possible referrals for your needs.

Is there something in their story you connect with?
Could you gain a new idea or insight for your business or career?
Who do you know or who do they know that can help both of you?
If you needed help or wanted to buy a product, what would it be?
How do you follow up when you meet someone?
When people view your profile, how do you want them to feel?
Do your tribes line up so you could be Power Partners?
What are your favorite questions to ask in an introductory call?

Michelle Price

**Chief Learning Officer
knows how Monetize Your Book
or Brain Online |
Social Media Savvy Influencer &
Superconnector**

"When you leverage your book, you will ultimately leverage yourself out from under the trading time for dollars trap, add more value to your work, and make a bigger impact with your message." ~ Michelle Price

You can only trade so much time for dollars. Leverage your book.

My life-long learning was inspired by weekly trips to the public library with my mother. I'd come home with stacks of books. At work, I learned how to systematically develop and deliver training programs. In the late nineties, I bought so much information I figured out packaging knowledge was how people were monetizing expertise online. My first client's book launched online to national best seller status but the real money was in the retreat workshop we did 90 days later. A client once told me I was being paid for my time. I instinctively replied that no, I was being paid for my value and what I knew. He agreed! We both learned something that day.

Today I coach and train women authors and experts to add value to their books by first creating and selling an online course, then a series of courses vs. selling more services.

▶ Women typically first use their book to sell more services because it's how they've been taught to use the book.

▶ Create an online course from your book first or create as you are writing the book

▶ This will begin to leverage your book to help you decrease time traded for dollars, plus add value and make more impact on your readers.

SPECIALTIES: ★Researching / Positioning / Designing / Developing / Training / Teaching / Online Course Sites / Social Media / Content Strategy / Thought Leadership Storyteller★

What three books do you feel are a must that you highly recommend others to read? *The Science of Getting Rich, Having It All, The Art of Original Thinking: The Making of a Thought Leader*

What movie touched you by its meaning or inspired you? Radio with Cuba Gooding, Jr.

Who in your childhood was a major influence that helped shape your life? My mother. She graduated from Dillard University in the forties, which was a major accomplishment back then. As children, she encouraged life-long learning, introduced my brothers and I to museums, plays and classical music. And she took us to the library every week.

What will you do differently this year from last year or what do you want more of? Take bigger risks.

If you could be anyone for a day, who would it be and what experience can you envision? Tony Robbins. Helping someone change their state immediately.

What discipline could someone learn from you? Curiosity. The art of asking really good questions. It's amazing what you can learn from others when you ask and then really listen.

If there were one problem in the world you could solve, what would it be? Self-limiting beliefs.

Michelle's Favorite Characteristics
Curious, connected, astute, innovative, resourceful, sense of humor, strategic, action-oriented

Michelle Price aka The Chief Book Monetizer at SellMoreBooks.com
Monetize your book to add more value, be more visible and make more impact!
▶ 619-717-2823 ▶ Michellep@SellMoreBooks.com ▶
www.SellMoreBooks.com ▶ www.SellMoreExpertise.com

Darrell Gurney

**Executive Career Transition Coach &
Licensed Spiritual Counselor Helping
Pros Land Dream Careers,
Skip HR & Negotiate**

"You have yet to do what you came here to do." --Darrell W. Gurney

An outgrowth of humble, blue-collar, Texas-country roots, I've studied and incorporated the worlds of work, personal development, and purposeful fulfillment. As an ambitious teenager, I was the first in my family to go to college and went on to graduate Summa Cum Laude from one of the world's best business schools, being named an Outstanding 7Student for school and community leadership. I then worked for a Big-8 consulting firm in London before returning to the US and landing in Los Angeles.

Today, combining what I retain from down-home roots and what I've learned through lifetime training and development, I bring a mix of easy demeanor and experienced wisdom to bear in supporting high-achieving individuals to grow

▶ 30-year track record of empowering, personally branding, and strategically positioning senior executives, entrepreneurs and MBA students to take the market by "backdoor" storm. Award-winning author of three career transformation books, teaching innovative and non-traditional paths to both passion self-discovery and thought-leader connectedness.

▶ Developed and established multiple coaching and training programs to empower women, senior executives, and mid-lifers to expand fully into their unique Self. BBW Coaching, PlayGame Coaching, and The Back Forty Coaching and programs all designed to cause playful, passionate, and purposeful second halves of career and life.

Specialties: Coaching: Career, Entrepreneurial, Effectiveness, Expansion / Corporate 360 Degree Consultation / Inspirational Speaking for MBA and Undergraduate Programs and Professional Groups / Personal Branding Expert / Badass Business Women Empowerment /

What three books do you feel are a must that you highly recommend others to read? The *War of Art* by Steven Pressfield, *Man's Search for Meaning* by Viktor Frankl, *A Course in Miracles* by Foundation for Inner Peace

What movie touched you by its meaning or inspired you? *Ghandi* 1982: The power of peaceful centeredness to move mountains.

What discipline could someone learn from you? How to live inside the gap created when one understands that becoming precedes results.

What subject or argument most stirs your emotions, why? What's really possible for people and in life. The arguments of limitation presented by the past, or how things have been, or how one knows oneself to be are life reducing. On the contrary, questions of "What if" and interactions which induce possibility outside of generally accepted conventions...those are conversations worth having.

If there were one problem in the world you could solve, what would it be? The hallucination of separation.

What is your purpose? Speaking, writing and coaching to infuse hope and possibility in a world that resists possibility.

How will you be spoken of in your eulogy? Passionately driven to make a difference, Darrell learned to get out of the way and let it happen through him. And the rest is history.

Darrell's Favorite Characteristics
Bold, Authentic, Possibility Thinker, Empowering, "Play First" Advocate (i.e., Go for it, before all the ducks are in a row! Get started!) Visionary, Purposeful

Darrell W. Gurney, aka "The Radical Possibilities Creator & Connector"
Founder, CareerGuy.com & TheBackForty.com, Inspirational Author, Speaker, Coach, & Program Leader
▶ Darrell@DarrellGurney.com ◀ and ▶ (310) 400-0647 ◀

"A vision without action is merely a dream. An action without vision just passes time. But, a vision with action can change the world."
--Joel Arthur Barker

I come from a family of survivors who lost everything and nearly everyone, not once, but twice. First the Holocaust and then the Hungarian revolution, and thrived in the free world. This is the foundation to a life that has enabled me to be who I am and to build a life and career that allows me to help others, especially entrepreneurs, expand their horizon and create opportunities for growth.

Today I run a vibrant event planning company that has produced extraordinary results for my global clients. Whether I'm designing or coordinating an event, consulting for, or distributing an independent film or TV show, finding talent or creating a new business enterprise, my business and personal philosophy is to act with integrity and honesty.

▶An amazing Crowd Funding portal that just launched --- I help you launch your project, work with you and make sure you succeed. I will speak at your event, teach you how to work on your project and so much more. I will even help you distribute it if your project qualifies

▶With over 10 years in the conference and events industry, clients and network range from Fortune 500 companies, women's organizations to non-profits and many associations,

▶As a recruiter I help you find the right candidate or the right job - referrals are the best way to find the top candidates and I look for referrals from my associates. I reconnect with the many companies I have worked with over the years with one of the top recruiting companies in California, I worked with many of the top companies and would like to link with them again. I would like to connect with other recruiters.

Specialties: Event Planning, Business Development, Film and TV Producer/Distributor, Crowdfunding consultant, Author, Speaker

What movie touched you by its meaning or inspired you? *The Wizard of Oz* - Specifically the lyrics to 'Somewhere Over the Rainbow'. It was written by the sons of immigrants from the world my family came from.

Who in your childhood was a major influence that helped shape your life? My mom was an inspiration by how she lived her life. Her strength made me strong and her sacrifices for her family made me believe that anything was possible.

Who is or has been a mentor, coach or strategist on your advisory board? Until his untimely death a few years ago, Frank Maguire, a founder of FedEx, was a wonderful mentor. He believed that anything you set your mind to is possible. His book, 'You're the Greatest' was the gift he left behind for me and the thousands of people whose lives he touched.

What discipline could someone learn from you, that could take them to the next level, and how did you develop it? Always doing too much at the same time, I worried that I wasn't doing my best for my clients or for myself. I now have the ability to focus fully on each project, giving it my full attention and finish what I start. I recognized my A-type personality and have adapted my multi-tasking skills to it.

In helping others, is it better to teach them, give them, or show them? All of the above. Depending on where the person is, you may have to give them some of what they need in order to prepare them to learn. When they're ready to learn, you apply the right approach - which may be showing, doing, or just throwing them into the deep end.

When winning someone over, do you think facts or emotions carry the day? Both. Facts are important because they provide context and credibility; But emotions are the ingredients that connect you to others. want to create a feeling of trust.

If there was one problem in the world you could solve, what would it be? To stop the lies, the corruption and the conflicts that destroys people's lives.

Aggie's Favorite Characteristics
Authentic, Collaborative, Ethical, Energetic, Hard Working, Honest, Connected, Accountable.

▶ 949.727.1211 ◀ Aggie@CECGlobalEvents.com
LinkedIn Profile: https://www.linkedin.com/in/aggiekobrin

We all construct worldviews
that give us a sense of meaning.

Mostly it is about
belonging to a group
and having a sense
of identity and purpose.

Carmen Lawrence

Chapter 6
Groups, Tribes, and Communities

There are 7 billion on the planet. There's enough business for everyone.

--Sandra Yancey

Sandra Yancey
Founder and CEO at eWomenNetwork, Inc.
Dallas/Fort Worth Area | Marketing and Advertising

Previous The Yancey Consulting Group, The Mead Corporation, Lexis-Nexis

Education Gestalt Institute

Send a message Endorse ▾ 500+
           connections

My Influencers: Sandra Yancey

Have you ever stopped at a long traffic light only to notice that there are far fewer cars in the lane next to you? The next time you stop at a light, you choose your lane more carefully and get through the light more quickly than the rest, who remain in that familiar trance state.

In the same way, when you join a group, try to connect with the leaders. Take a few extra minutes to find out the name of the group Founder/Owner. This will give you an extra edge. If the group is important enough to join, it is important enough to read the group profile and see who created it. The group owner is a leader who may know many people that you want to know. You can click on their names and look through their profiles to see if you want to connect with them.

93

Belonging to a group or organization that aligns with like-minded people opens many doors. My best friend Lori Hart, the Celebrity Makeup Artist, introduced me to Sara Michaels at a conference in Las Vegas. Sara, president of the Los Angeles chapter of eWomenNetwork, was having a luncheon and Founder-President Sandra Yancey was coming.

Because I was booked, I looked at Sandra's LinkedIn profile. She was named an American Hero by CNN and had international awards for making a difference than I had ever seen. She created eWomenNetwork, one of the largest and most decorated business organizations in North America, a multi-million-dollar enterprise in six countries with 118 chapters helping thousands of women grow their businesses

She has won many international business and charity awards. The eWomenNetwork Foundation she created has awarded cash grants to 94 non-profit organizations and scholarships to 132 emerging female leaders. "Unlike in school," she says, "in life you don't have to come up with all the right answers. You can ask the people around you for help — or even ask them to do the things you don't do well."

I did make it to the luncheon, asked a few engaging questions and created a conversation that could be continued. I followed up with a thank you and an invite to connect on LinkedIn. Never be shy to connect with leaders. They are natural connectors and want to broaden their own networks.

Consider adding her to your influencer list.

Seven Ways to Pick a Group

Being part of the right group has always been an important part of our identity and is an important part of LinkedIn as well. Being associated with the right group can help you land the right job!

If you look at Mike Ferry™'s LinkedIn page, you will see that he has joined a lot of groups that include realtors. This makes a lot of sense if, like Mike, you are one of the top real estate professional trainers in the world. However, it makes no sense at all if you are a real estate agent. Many agents make a huge mistake when they create their LinkedIn profiles. They join groups made up of other realtors. They think that by being visible in the realtor community, they will attract customers. What is the mistake? When you do this, other realtors will find you and look at your profile. Nobody else will. The most important question you can ask yourself, the question that means everything for you and your business, is, "Is a realtor going to sell a house to another realtor?" Rephrase this question so it applies to your business.

Searching for groups is very simple on LinkedIn. The search bar allows you the find People, Updates, Jobs, Companies, your Inbox, or Groups. You want to make Groups your default. Just change your settings.

LinkedIn is home to over 2,000,000 groups. Groups representing every industry, hobby, life interest and passion can be found on LinkedIn. Picking a group is like picking music. With so many genres available, it is critical that you chose the ones that fit your purpose in your profession but also in your personality and gifts. Here are some options:

What tribes are is a very simple concept that goes back 50 million years. It's about leading and connecting people and ideas. And it's something that people have wanted forever.
--Seth Godin

---

1. Group Size - Papa Bear, Mama Bear, and Baby Bear: (this is a fun metaphor that I use to remember group size)
  A. The first thing you want to select when you are picking a group is to pick a huge group, the Papa Bear
  B. Then pick a medium-sized group, the Mama Bear
  C. Then add a small group, the Baby Bear

2. Fun-Fun-Fun: Of the 2,000,000 groups on LinkedIn, pick a fun, exciting group that makes you think, "Wow, if I could do this for a living, this would be fun."

3. Recruit Me. I want a job: Find out where all the Human Resources people, recruiters and headhunters play. Seek them out and speak to them.

4. People like Me: Find groups with people like you that you can ask, "What works for you and what doesn't."

FENG: 1st level #61, 2nd level #327

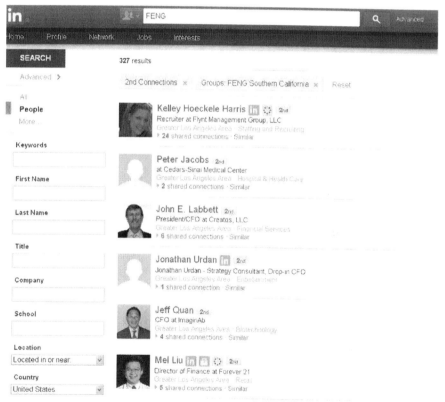

5. Who are your Top 25? Look at their groups and join groups that make sense for you.

6. Job Groups, Headhunters, and Recruiters: Joining these groups is the key to successful searches for recruiters who live in your community or are recruiters for your industry or field

7. Top Link: I have saved the Best for Last. This open Networkers Group (TopLink.com) has 138,000 members. If you are not yet a member, you can click the "Join Group" button. This open networker group includes some of the very largest connectors on LinkedIn, many of whom have many thousands of connections. When you first join this group, let the Open Networkers Logo show up on your profile since it might attract more connections interested in what you do. In the future, however, when you reach a higher level on LinkedIn and want to show only high-quality groups in your profile, do not show the TopLink Logo because it means that you're an open connector. If want to keep your connections more private and want them to look at you as a careful connector with special people, you don't want them to know you are an open networker.

Do make it a practice to explore the many groups on LinkedIn. Before you join any group, you can see the members of the group who are in your network and in some groups you can read discussion threads. At the very least, you can see who the group owner is, how many members the group has, and whether it is open or closed. Once you join, you can see the other people who belong to the group.

When you see the five or six connections of yours that are members of the new group, you might think, "Oh my goodness, all of these people are first connections with me. These individuals have (for instance) painting careers but I'm not in this group with them." If you see that six of your first level connections are in this art group and you are interested in art, you might want to pursue stronger connections with those people."

You do want to join the maximum of 50 groups because when you are in a group, you can send up to 15 emails per month to individual members of a group without being connected to them. This opens up a few more people who can send you a message.

However, work just the top three of these groups strongly so you do not make extra work for yourself. Work smarter, not harder.

What's a tribe?

If you look up the word "tribe" in the dictionary you will get this definition: a social division in a traditional society consisting of families or communities linked by social, economic, religious, or blood ties, with a common culture and dialect, typically having a recognized leader.

In order to effect great change, we need to look at how we can help those in our own communities as well as globally.
--Christina Aguilera

Your most important job on LinkedIn is to find others in your field. Begin by looking at 100 people who do what you do on LinkedIn. You will see how they target their tribe and you will find good connections who could refer business to you. I've looked at thousands of profiles, so I have a good idea what a successful profile contains. If you haven't looked at your first 100 people, then you have no idea who is out there and who can help you.

Keep a notebook labeled *Tips and Ideas for LinkedIn*. When you find people who might be good connections, make a note of them. Write down how that person resonates with you and what that person might mean to you. Then connect with them.

When you do connect with your new contacts, the most critical thing you can do is acknowledge them. Before you connect, the button beside the profile picture says, "Connect." After you connect, it says, "Send a message." When I connect with another person, one of the key things I do is click that button and send them a message thanking them for connecting with me. This is the best way to build relationships on LinkedIn and it takes just 60 seconds.

Group Etiquette & Settings

Did your grandma ever tell you to take your elbows off the table? How about which fork to use to eat the salad? And how many times have you been told not to talk with your mouth full? These are all forms of etiquette. Believe it or not, forms of etiquette exist in dealing with groups on LinkedIn as well. Many realtors will jump into just realtor groups. Job seekers do the same thing. They jump into every Job group they can find.

Social media is not about the exploitation of technology but service to community.
--Simon Mainwaring

When a visitor looks at your profile and sees groups focused on job seekers, they think that if they reach out to you, all you will want from them is a job.

One time I was in a real estate office talking with a friend and another person walked in the door. All of a sudden 30 agents in the office picked up the phone.

I said to my friend, "What the heck was that? I just saw 90% of the agents grab the phone and stick it to their ear."

My friend laughed and said, "Yeah, that man who walked in is a title company representative. The agents put the phone to their ear so the title person wouldn't stop at their desk to talk to them. It is their way of avoiding telling him they are too busy to talk."

The same thing can happen on LinkedIn. When you put the wrong group logos on your profile, many people will not want to connect with or talk to you. The best way to avoid this is to hide the group logos that aren't attractive to your viewers.

When you set up your group membership settings, make sure to unclick two items, your logo for the groups you don't want others to see and your digest, unless the group is one of your top three, in which case you want to get every message everybody is sending because this is your tribe. You don't want every message from the other 49 groups. Unclick the daily digest if you don't want to get daily or weekly messages. However, always click the bottom two buttons which allow the Group Manager to send you email and other members to send you messages.

For digest emails, you have a choice of weekly or daily emails. A very busy person will unclick both of those for all but a few groups. You can change the settings from a daily notice to a weekly notice if you prefer. For groups where there is too much chatter, don't allow digest messages.

Diversify Your Groups

Entrepreneurs

Executives - Boomers - **Entrepreneurs** [Member]
Former CMC, Now...Executives-Boomers-**Entrepreneurs**! We focus to assist each other in developing lifetime relationships &...
1,147 members
Similar

OnStartups · On Startups - The Community For **Entrepreneurs**
Startup community for **entrepreneurs** and small business owners. If you're an entrepreneur, you should join the largest ...
543,337 members
Similar

small
BUSINESS · Small Business Network: Startups & **Entrepreneurs** talk Social Media Marketing Startup Jobs Sales PR
Small Business Network is for the entrepreneur founder & owner. **Entrepreneurs** who startup grow SMB & SMEs. Discuss online ...
114,009 members
Similar

A Startup Specialists Group - Online Network for **Entrepreneurs** and Startups (Business Jobs Careers)
Venture Capital Investors Angels VC IT Digital Tech Finance Media Social Legal Mobile Pharma Biotech Cloud PR Legal in ...
205,555 members
Similar

Groups are like the Super Bowl 50

It seems almost unpatriotic not to watch the Super Bowl so I turned on the game and thought, "No way" when I saw it was the big one, Number 50. Who hasn't watched a super bowl? It's the #1 American game of the year. To be ironic, Carlos Santana sang and played. It brought back a lot of memories.

We all want to win but it is how we play the game. In groups you must pick the ones you relate to, know it has the people you want to play with, and that it is the place you're willing to invest some time in. When you are post an article, you wrote or one you want to share, ask yourself, "Is there alignment my values and needs."

Here are This Chapter's Business Consultant Influencers

As you read these profiles, look for possible referrals for your needs.

Is there something in their story you connect with?

Could you gain a new idea or insight for your business or career?

Who do you know or who do they know that can help both of you?

If you needed help or wanted to buy a product, what would it be?

How do you follow up when you meet someone?

When people view your profile, how do you want them to feel?

Do your tribes line up so you could be Power Partners?

What are your favorite questions to ask in an introductory call?

Francesca Gallo

CEO / Founder
Bella Mare Retreats For Executives
& MasterMinds /
Show Producer at Brides Du Jour
/ Advisor London Busses

Let the beauty of what you love be what you do. ~ Rumi

Born and raised in Brooklyn NY with a big Italian family My grandparents were extremely industrious they bought a brownstone where your business is downstairs & you lived above. By 22 my entrepreneurial spirit took me to California which started my real estate journey. Next organized & produced Bridal shows black tux it was a fit for a black London Taxis. This grew into owning and operating the first British double decker bus company in Los Angeles which transported the LA Lakers in their championship parades.

Today I organize retreats in unique places bringing groups together from all over the world. I am known as the Couture Connector because I bring the best of the best in retreats with health and wellness. If you or your company are ready for your next level let's talk success.

▶Speakers... Are you looking for a location to bring your high-end clients to have the best mastermind experience or intimate venue, We take the worries away by providing unique properties Our staff provides all the organizing from meals, spa treatments & recreation fun like ie. hiking, canoeing, fishing & etc

▶Looking for a venue for your next corporate retreat... Why not Bella Mare Retreat-Laguna Beach. Nothing recharges executive burnout than a fresh landscape, new mindset will reset & recharge.

▶Friends Getaway Retreat; whether it is for fun or a mindfulness wellness. From nutritious meals, meditations, yoga etc. It's a mind, body and spirit rejuvenated experience to reach yourself.

SPECIALTIES: Facilitate Retreats / Friends & Vacation Getaway / Corporate Executive Retreats / Men or Women ReUnions / 6 Day BootCamps & Transformational Retreats / 3 Day Therapeutic Healing

What three books do you feel are a must that you highly recommend others to read? Power of the Mind, Tony Robbins, Cyber...Cybernetics...

Who in your childhood was a major influence that helped shape your life? Growing up with grandparents and parents who were very entrepreneurial minded and savvy business people.

With what "LinkedIn Influencer" do you resonate and what character trait do you share? Deborah Faris...the character trait we share is perseverance....

What will you do differently this year from last year or what do you want more of? The thing I would do different from last year is travel more...

Who now is a Mentor, Coach or Strategist that is on your advisory council? Deborah Faris...

What discipline could someone learn from you? Patience...

When "winning someone over" do you think facts or emotions carry the day? Facts....

What movie makes you cry, every time you see it? An Affair To Remember....

If there were one problem in the world you could solve, what would it be? Bringing people together without discrimination of race, religion, or gender...

Francesca's Favorite Characteristics
Facilitates, Authentic, Collaborative, Couture, Integrity

Francesca Gallo aka "Matching Individuals with their Perfect Retreats"
CEO & Founder Bella Mare Retreats "Where Sanctuary Brings Productivity"
Helping people to regain, recharge, re-set their mind & body!
▶ FrancescaUSA52@gmail.com ◀
▶ 818-451-8883 ◀ ▶ www.BellaMareRetreat.com

Randy Hausauer

Get the Green
Your Business Needs to Grow!
Visit AllGreenFunding.com &
Explore all Real Estate & Business Loans

"Do what you love in the service of those who love what you do."
~ Steve Farber

When I was young I became a corporate attorney because, according to my mom, of my ability to argue. After I received a BS in Financial Investments & Real Estate, to pay for law school, I joined a major stock firm, but wasn't helping others. A police ride-a-long led me to join the Long Beach PD for 29 years, where I was Detective in the Major Fraud Unit, Supervisor and Manager of the Gang Unit and Manager of Emergency Preparedness, including operational responsibility for possible terrorist targets. This and playing football through college, flipping houses and being on the board of a few charities prepared me for what I'm doing now.

Today, our team has structured over $500 Million in Small Business Loan Transactions. We help Business Owners, Entrepreneurs, Professionals, and Real Estate Investors obtain the money to grow their business. Our connections my clients get funding where others can't.

▶ Business Owners, Entrepreneurs. Creative Funding for Growth.

▶ Start Up Funding. Performance Based, No Up-Front Fees.

▶ Real Estate Investors. House Flipping. No Obligation to Pre-Qualify.

I believe in giving back. I chaired the Kathy Ireland Teen Mother Mentoring Program and am part of an annual Christmas program for disenfranchised children and 911 For Kids/Athletes and Entertainers.

SPECIALTIES: SBA Green Loans / Business Loans / Commercial Real Estate Lending / Private Money / Broker Revenue Share / Real Estate Investor Loans/ Rental Portfolio Loans / Startup's up to 500k Unsecured Funding low as 8% / Funding Consulting / Bridge Loans / Credit Lines / Funding in as little as 10 Days

What three books do you feel are a must that you highly recommend others to read? *Man's Search for Meaning,* Viktor Frankl; *Think and Grow Rich*, Napoleon Hill; *How to Win Friends and Influence People*, Dale Carnegie. These three books combined provide a clear message that we have a freedom of choice as to how we handle our own circumstances and that never losing hope is key.

What movie touched you by its meaning or inspired you? I was touched by the movie *The Shawshank Redemption*. The message about hope is strong for the main character Andy despite overwhelming odds.

Who in your childhood was a major influence that helped shape your life? My father was a major influencer in my life. He showed me how to respect others and their opinions even if I didn't agree with them. Also taught me integrity and how important it is to have the trust of others.

In helping others, is it better to teach them, give them, or show them? With respect to helping others, I subscribe to the Chinese Proverb: Give a man a fish and you feed him for a day. Teach a man to fish and you feed him for a lifetime. I believe that teaching and showing go hand and hand.

If there were one problem in the world you could solve, what would it be? To provide clean water for all.

When "winning someone over" do you think facts or emotions carry the day? I think emotions carry the day. I think most people make decisions based on how that decision will make them feel. Understanding this has helped me to improve both my personal and my business relationships.

What will you do differently this year from last year or what do you want more of? I will become more purposeful this year focusing on the 20% that yield 80% of the results I want. This is really important to me so that I can spend more time focusing on myself and my individual goals.

Randy's Favorite Characteristics

Integrity, Tenacious, Responsible, Committed, Determined, Passionate, Trustworthy, Nurturing, Optimistic, Adventurous, Compassionate

Randy Hausauer aka *"The Funding Connector"*
"Get the Green Your Business Needs to Grow!"
♛ SBA Green Loans ♛ Real Estate Investor Loans ♛ Startup's up to 500k
Unsecured Funding as Low as 8% ♛ Private Money
♟ Randy@AllGreenFunding.com ♟ 562.480.5582 ♛
www.AllGreenFunding.com ✓

"Leadership is influence, nothing more, nothing less." ~ John Maxwell

As a child I was challenged by severe stuttering, and I was extremely quiet around others. It took until I was 21 and serving in the United States Air Force with the 305th SFS as a K9 handler to learn how to be comfortable in my own vulnerability when I developed a relationship and talked to my dog.

Later as a Police Officer with the City of Jackson, Mississippi I had to make a split-second decision on whether or not to take a perpetrators life during an altercation. I decided against it and resigned with two-weeks notice. In that moment of clarity, I realized that my purpose in life is to develop and encourage vulnerable leadership.

Today, I'm a certified speaker/coach with the John Maxwell Leadership Team and founder of my own company, Leaders 4 Leaders, LLC. I continue to work nationally with the best and brightest in the leadership development field.

▶ Tenured Executives with a desire to operate within their purpose
▶ C-Level Executives who have an unfulfilled passion
▶ Higher Educated Professionals with positions that aren't commensurate with their degree/s

Specialties: Leadership Speaking / Training and Facilitating / Motivational Speaking / Executive Coaching / Corporate Facilitator

Who in your childhood was a major influence that helped shape your life? The major influencer during my childhood was my mother, Lisa Faussette. She taught me the value of self-respect, hard work and belief in self no matter the circumstances.

If you could be anyone for a day, who would it be and what experience can you envision? If I could be anyone for a day, I'd be "ME", a decade from today. I envision speaking to an audience of thousands about the benefits of VULNERABILITY with my wife and children by my side.

What discipline could someone learn from you? The discipline someone can learn from me, would be learning how to have FUN! We must first understand that things and people will never bring us the happiness that we desire most. Once we bridge the gap between our mind and our heart, we can then move towards a life of FUN!

Dom's Favorite Characteristics

Grit, Determination, Forward Thinker, Passionate Speaker, Integral, Servant Leadership, service before self, relatable, good listener, compassionate

Dom Faussette aka *"Speaking Cadre"*
"CONNECT WITH YOUR AUTHENTIC PURPOSE.THINK. REACT. LEAD"
♕ Leadership Speaker ♕ Motivational Speaker ♕ Corporate Facilitator
♕ Executive Coach
♖ thinkreactlead@gmail.com 📱602-481-0650 ♕
www.thinkreactlead.com ✓

People are not remembered
by how few times they fail,

but by how often
they succeed.

Every Wrong Step
is another step forward.

Thomas Edison

Chapter 7
Follow-Up and Follow-Through

Taking the first step is the difference between actually pursuing your passion and just dreaming about it.

--Jack Canfield

Jack Canfield

CEO, The Canfield Training Group | Speaker | Coach |
NY Times Bestselling Author

Santa Barbara, California | Professional Training & Coaching

Current	Transformational Leadership Council, The Canfield Training Group, Over 250 convention and association meetings worldwide
Previous	Chicken Soup for the Soul Enterprises
Education	Canadian Institute for Psychosynthesis

Send a message ▾

500+
connections

My Influencers: Jack Canfield

We all love chicken soup for the soul series but few of us know the story behind its success. A few years ago, I was at Rick Frishman's Author 101 event, where Jack Canfield gave one of the keynotes. Jack was part of the team that created *Chicken Soup for The Soul* in the early 1990's. In his talk he told how he and Mark Victor Hanson shopped the book around to over 140 publishers before a tiny house in Virginia decided to publish it. They were ecstatic that the book was published but decided they wanted to make it a true best seller.

Now this is very difficult. Only a few books ever get that distinction. So Jack and Mark came up with a plan. They would do three things every day to promote the book. Publishing was nice, they knew, but even 95% of commercially published books sell few to no copies. They did speeches, book signings, travels around the county, television shows, radio shows and more radio shows. Even with that amount of promotion, it took almost a year. The book gradually caught on, then sales shot up as word of mouth took over. By the one-year mark, the book was a number one New York Times best seller.

However, they didn't stop there. Follow-up is the key to true success so they brought out a second book, *A Second Helping of Chicken Soup for the Soul*. It sold as well. Now they knew they were onto something big. Book followed book over the years, on every subject you could imagine, over 130 titles in the next 23 years.

The series, rejected by nearly every publisher in the country, languishing on bookshelves for the better part of a year, became one of the highest selling series of all time at 130 million copies, all because Jack and Mark followed up, followed up, and followed up in their search for a publisher, in their march to best-seller status, and in their creation of additional titles in the series.

They could have given up after the first 10 rejections but didn't and that disciplined follow-through resulted in overwhelming success.

Consider adding him to your influencer list.

Follow-up is a Winners Game

There can be a thousand excuses why a potential contact didn't follow up with you or you didn't follow up with a new acquaintance. Either way, when follow-up doesn't happen ask yourself how your potential contact might like to be followed up with, either by phone, text, or e-mail. If you don't know, find out!

Some people may get 200 emails a day, some people have an assistant who handles their emails and that gatekeeper may have already recycled you. Don't call a person during non-business hours if you are not a personal friend because you have no personal connection. On the other hand, if you're going to meet with them at a charity run on the weekend, an after-hours call may be appropriate. If you are calling someone on a Sunday and they have Sunday reserved as a family day, you lose relationship currency.

Thoughts and Tips

Make it easy for your friends to find you.

Create your customized LinkedIn profile name.

Texting is another tricky subject. One time I was doing a favor for some people by updating their profiles on LinkedIn. When I finished, I let them know that the profile was changed and asked them to go in and check it out. I didn't hear anything from them right away so I went on with other things and figured we would catch up later. I didn't mean 3:30 a.m.! In the middle of the night, when I was fast asleep, my cell phone started squawking. OMG...who could be texting me at this horrible hour! It must be an emergency! Startled and confused, I got out of bed to check the message. What did I find? A text from one of the team members I was working with on the LinkedIn site, telling me about grammar mistakes and spelling errors. "Are you kidding me?" I thought. "It's 3:30 a.m. and they woke me up to tell me that?" I was not happy.

Remember, timing is everything. Be aware of what you're sending, when you're sending it, and how professional the content you're sending is. It can make a huge difference.

Another lesson I learned is that the bigger the person you want to contact, the more cautious and strategic you need to be in your follow-up. Asking them repeatedly for a connection or conversation will only tick them off. Once you make this mistake, you have created a negative relationship that could haunt you for years. Look at the big picture. If you are a screenwriter on a project that could take years, maybe your follow-up would be every other month. Base your follow-up timing on the players in your game of chess.

The best follow-up on LinkedIn is to send an invite. If they accept, send a thank you note and send your next step, which usually turns into a phone call opportunity. From the phone call, the next step is to meet in person. From there, take steps as the situation warrants. For instance, if you are in medical sales and you planned to meet a doctor to play a round of golf, consider the possible commission from that meeting and the possible referrals that doctor could give you to new doctors or hospitals that might use your company's products. What if that commission was worth $10,000? Ask yourself how you would approach that client. The answer is clear: Ask that client for an appointment and follow up with them. Treat them like gold. Most people miss these opportunities because they don't realize the potential of a simple first meeting. The first impression they make kills the future possibility.

Reach Out and Touch Someone

In sales we have a follow up system we call the "14 touch points." In some industries, sales representatives drop off a card and a Payday candy bar. It sounds silly and simple, but consider this scenario. If it was 3 p.m. on a Friday afternoon and you loved Payday candy bars and you returned to the office to find a Payday sitting on your desk waiting for you, you would be very excited. When you notice that your sales representative delivered it because he remembered a conversation where you said you loved them, it leaves a positive feeling. You knew he was in a different city on Fridays and must have driven to your city just to drop of the candy bar before heading back to his office to turn in his required Friday reports. He just made himself your favorite rep and the next time you need to order his product you will remember him! That 50-cent candy bar might just have made him a nice commission.

If your imagination leads you to understand how quickly people grant your requests when those requests appeal to their self-interest, you can have practically anything you go after.
--Napoleon Hill

Ask, Ask, Ask for Help and Referrals

The biggest challenge that is I see people have when they network is also one of the three biggest challenges people have in communication. This is true for everyone, male or female, young or old. They have great difficulty saying:

1. I love you
2. I'm sorry
3. Can you help me?

Be larger than your task.
--Orison Sweet Marden

We seem to forget our purpose when we are networking. For example, if you are looking for a job, after you have identified your contact and built a relationship, you must be clear when you request help and ask specifically what you are looking for. The key is to ask! If you want the person to introduce you to an important executive....ask! If you want to connect through LinkedIn to a CEO at a company you want to work for, ask for an introduction. Use your connections to your benefit. "Can you connect me with John Smith? He's the Vice President of Merchandising and I'm thinking about applying there in six months." Send two simple sentences to someone in your network who knows John Smith and who knows, you might just get an interview.

Companies

USA TODAY
Newspapers
✓ Following

American Marketing ...
Marketing and Advertising
✓ Following

Umpqua Bank
Banking
✓ Following

Verizon
Information Technology
and Services
✓ Following

OCEAN BANK

Ocean Bank
Banking
✓ Following

AV Event Solutions
Events Services
✓ Following

Peak Potentials
Professional Training &
Coaching
✓ Following

National College Plan...
Education Management
✓ Following

Sears Home Services
Consumer Services
✓ Following

Boston Private Bank
Banking
✓ Following

Udemy
E-Learning
✓ Following

Chevron

Chevron
Oil & Energy
✓ Following

Dell
Information Technology
and Services
✓ Following

Socal BNI
Professional Training &
Coaching
✓ Following

Dale Carnegie Training
Professional Training &
Coaching
✓ Following

HDFC Bank
Banking
✓ Following

Who are your Top Five Companies?

In networking, part of your pitch is to share what company you would like to work for. Even more important than your pitch is your follow-up. Make a list of five to seven different ways you can share your mission with people. Ask yourself why you want to work for them. Re-read the job description and find out what they are looking for. Tailor your follow-up specifically to what they want.

Only one thing…a desire so strong, a determination so intense, that you cheerfully throw everything you have into the scale to win what you want. Not merely your work and your money and your thought, but the willingness to stand or fall by the result — to do or to die.

--Robert Collier

Example:

Dear Mr. Brown,

I am in retiring from my current job in three months. I have started to identify possible part-time jobs and companies that interest me. In my search, I found your marketing position and would like to discuss the possibility of applying for this job before I retire. I want to thank you in advance for the opportunity and ask that if you know of anyone or any LinkedIn group that can help me on my path, please share my information with them and help me on my mission.

Thank you again for accepting my LinkedIn invite.

I hope to be an added contributor to many others in the future.

Signed by you

(Your current email address)

(Your current phone number)

Identify the top five companies you want to work for. Research them and identify jobs within these organizations that interest you. Find the names of people in these organizations and see if they are on LinkedIn. If so, see if anyone you're connected to is connected to them. Search the actual companies on LinkedIn and see if they have a LinkedIn presence or have available jobs listed. Many companies use LinkedIn to list job opportunities. Find out everything you can about the five companies you have identified and become a top candidate for them.

Identify your Top 20 Connections

> *It was character that got us out of bed, commitment that moved us into action, and discipline that enabled us to follow through.*
> **--Zig Ziglar**

Have you ever met a person and later said to yourself, "I wish I had followed up or I should have stayed in touch with…" When I was in my 20s, a real estate broker said to me, "If you have 100 people who like you, know you and trust you, you won't be looking for a job or a friend."

> *Marketing is not an event, but a process… It has a beginning, a middle, but never an end, for it is a process. You improve it, perfect it, change it, even pause it. But you never stop it completely.*
> **--J. Conrad Levinson**

As life passes, we see many changes along our path. Friends move, we move, we lose touch. One of my challenges was that after 30 years I hadn't keep in touch with many of my early contacts. I had missed many opportunities.

There's a saying I like a lot: "You can save a lot of time (time is money) if you learn from someone else's mistake." LinkedIn makes it easy to stay in touch with people, even those you lost contact with long ago. In the section on connecting, I showed you a memory jogger that helps you rediscover people you met in your past and recent present.

Begin by making a list of people you have connected with at your various jobs. The memory jogger will also help when you do your CRM (Client Retention Management).

You can use this as you develop your 100 top people. Since you are new at developing your relationships, this list will shift based on how future relationships and alignments develop as you meet more people.

I believe that you can get everything in life you want if you will just help enough other people get what they want.
--Zig Ziglar

Here is the recipe for who could be good resources for job connections: Four recruiters, Four alumni, Four current employees, and Four people from groups.

President Reagan wrote Five Thank You notes a day

Ronald Reagan was the 40th President of the United States and was one of our oldest presidents. Prior to his presidency, he served as the 33rd Governor of California. When he ran for office a common comment was, "Is this a joke?" because he had been on radio, television and in movies. Could a celebrity really run the country?

Not only was President Reagan one of our favorite presidents, he also had a gift for connecting with people. His style was to make connections personal so that people never forgot him. One of his professional business habits was to write five thank-you notes every day.

We keep moving forward opening new doors and doing new things, because we're curious and curiosity keeps leading us down new paths.
--Walt Disney

On LinkedIn, writing a thank-you is a wonderful way to start your relationships with new connections. When you say "thank you" and acknowledge your new LinkedIn friend or future colleagues, you are well on your way to building a personal relationship with them.

Here are This Chapter's Business Consultant Influencers

As you read these profiles, look for possible referrals for your needs.

Is there something in their story you connect with?

Could you gain a new idea or insight for your business or career?

Who do you know or who do they know that can help both of you?

If you needed help or wanted to buy a product, what would it be?

How do you follow up when you meet someone?

When people view your profile, how do you want them to feel?

Do your tribes line up so you could be Power Partners?

What are your favorite questions to ask in an introductory call?

"Your connections to all the things around you literally define who you are." ~ Aaron D. O'Connell

As a single dad in my early twenties I was motivated for success. Fortunately, I found a mentor who taught me the art and science of referrals. Over the past two decades I have been blessed to have closed over $500 million in transactions by referral.

Today I empower nearly 5 million business owners and professionals with our proven training, tools and technology at Refer.com. I focus on helping our members create profitable partnerships and generate raving referrals, so you close more sales with less effort.

Refer.com is a powerful Referral Marketing System that helps you grow a trusted referral network to assist you in filling your sales pipeline with warm leads... we currently have nearly 5 million members in over 200 countries. Our proven referral marketing system helps you:

▶ **PROMOTE** yourself and your partners through our 21 cross promotion campaigns.

▶ **TEAM UP** with complementary professionals who already serve your ideal clients every day.

▶ **ENGAGE** your best referrals sources effectively and consistently so you stay top of mind and become the go-to professional for your entire social sphere.

SPECIALTIES: Referral Marketing / Joint Ventures / Affiliate Sales / Lead Generation / Cross Promotion Campaigns / Referral Rewards / Elite Introductions / Empowering Events / Masterful Masterminds / Strategic Networking / Sensational Speaking / Profitable Partnerships / Enlightened Alliances / Superior Sponsorships / Creating Charity Champions

What three books do you feel are a must that you highly recommend others to read? *The One Minute Millionaire* is my favorite business book. Written by my personal mentor Mark Victor Hansen along with Robert Allen, this book will teach you "the enlightened way to wealth" so you design your life to create impact on top of income. Jack Canfield's *Success Principles* and Napoleon Hill's *Think and Grow Rich* are also must reads.

What movie touched you by its meaning or inspired you? *Pay It Forward* is one of the most meaningful movies of all times and gives the blueprint for uplifting and transforming humanity. The greatest gift you can receive is the satisfaction of helping someone else.

Who in your childhood was a major influence that helped shape your life? My drama and choir teachers. They gave me the courage and confidence to share my voice and shine my light to the world.

If you could have any superpower (or be any superhero), what/who would it be and why? A Love beam. I realize it sounds a little woo-woo, but I'd love to be able to shoot a beam from my eyes that would envelop people in light and fill them with overwhelming love, acceptance and appreciation.

What subject or argument most stirs your emotions, why? Charity. I'm on a mission to double global philanthropy to $1 trillion by the year 2020. I believe every business owner and professional should be a champion for charities that are important to them and aligned with their business

On what topic at parties would you really like to "get into it"? Besides charity, my passion is teaching people about Bitcoin and cryptocurrencies. So few people understand cryptocurrencies and I love enlightening people on how the blockchain works. Over the next 10 years, Bitcoin and other crypto coins will completely transform our financial system.

If there were one problem in the world you could solve, what would it be? I believe education is the biggest opportunity for uplifting our world. I'm not talking about simple reading, writing and arithmetic, but empowering education to create your ideal outcome.

Brandon's Favorite Characteristics
Generous, Compassionate, Empathetic, Optimistic, Passionate,
Adventurous, Integrous, Connected, Peaceful, Wise

Brandon Barnum ~ Powering the Referral Economy
Creating Real Business in the Real World "Relationships Matter"
► support@refer.com ◄ & ► 855-228-6824 ◄ ► www.Refer.com

Cory MichaelSanchez

Speaker / Author / CEO
B2B Lead Generation
Co-Founder Mojo Global
and ACK! The Book

If people like you, they'll listen to you, but if they trust you, they'll do business with you. ~ Zig Ziglar

When I was a kid, I always felt like a hero in a zero's body. I was painfully shy in high school and had few friends. Talking to girls was absolutely out of the question. I was desperate for change so I made an out of the box decision to enter the high school "Man Pageant" my senior year...a beauty pageant for dudes, to confront shyness and get out of my comfort zone.

I ended up losing the competition, but "doing it" put me on the map

I enjoyed a newfound "celebrity" like status that I'd never experienced before...all because I got out of my comfort zone and challenged myself.

Today, I'm a Co-Founder of Mojo Global, was awarded Phoenix Business Journal's "Marketer of the Year", achieved Top 1% of LinkedIn Influencers, have co-authored four books and been featured in Forbes on my mission to empower entrepreneurs globally. My wife and I recently published ACK! The book which launched a movement to spread the simple secret of how to beat bad days and live a happy joy-filled life.

▶ Safe, Secure, and Predictable Leads for Your Business

▶ Build a Loyal list of Raving Fans

▶ Close Large Transactions on Demand

Specialties: B2B Lead Generation, 100% Done-For-You Managed B2B Lead Generation Campaigns, Marketing, International Speaker, Best Selling Author

♛ B2B Lead Generation ♛ 100% Done-For-You Managed B2B Lead Generation Campaigns ♛ Best Selling Author ♛ International Speaker

♟ cory@mojoglobal.com ♟ 480-339-4300 ♛ www.mojoglobal.com

Tough times never last, but tough people do. ~ Robert H. Schuller

The love of personal fitness and sports is a constant in my life and has helped me amass over 100,000 miles running in marathons. I'm a former Championship High School and Collegiate Wrestler and member of the US Olympic Wrestling team. Through sports I learned the importance of being a team player, building perseverance, discipline and preparation.

Although I've created, run and sold numerous multi-million-dollar companies (even in the most brutal markets) one of my core values is community service. I am on the Board of Directors for Smiles Behind Bars which has helped over 200 previously incarcerated men and women restore their smiles and experience renewed confidence and self-esteem.

Today I'm the co-founder of Mojo Global with clients in over 30 countries. We've CRACKED the CODE on B2B Marketing and Lead Generation and have created a proprietary program of powerful systems and battle tested strategies that fills your calendar with affluent, laser beam targeted leads daily.

▶ Safe, Secure, and Predictable Leads for Your Business
▶ Build a Loyal list of Raving Fans
▶ Close Large Transactions on Demand

SPECIALTIES: B2B Lead Generation, 100% Done-For-You Managed B2B Lead Generation Campaigns, Marketing, International Speaker, Best Selling Author

Ira Rosen aka "The Billion Dollar Man"

♛ B2B Lead Generation ♚ 100% Done-For-You Managed B2B Lead Generation Campaigns ♛ Best Selling Author ♚ International Speaker

♟ ira@MojoGlobal.com ♜ 480-339-4300 ♛ www.MojoGlobal.com✓

You cannot change the world,

But you can present the world with one improved person -- Yourself.

You can go to work on yourself to make yourself

Into the kind of person you admire and respect.

You can become a role model and set a standard for others.

You can control and discipline yourself to resist acting

Or speaking in a negative way

Toward anyone for any reason.

You can insist upon always doing things the loving way,

Rather than the hurtful way.

By doing these things each day,

You can continue on your journey

Toward becoming an exceptional human being.

Brian Tracy

Chapter 8
Recommendations, Marketing

Customer satisfaction is worthless. Customer loyalty is priceless.
--Jeff Gitomer

Jeffrey Gitomer   PREMIUM
Best-Selling Author | Keynote Speaker | America's #1 Sales Authority | King of
Sales
Charlotte, North Carolina Area | Professional Training & Coaching
Current   Outstand, Buy Gitomer
Education Temple University

Send a message ▼   29,529
                                                         followers

My Influencers: Jeff Gitomer

Have you ever met a real book lover? We are kind of funny in our own ways. For me, if I am crazy about a book like "Think and Grow Rich", I would pick it up at the used book store for fifty cents and keep extra's in the car, to give to someone who was thirsty for knowledge. It gives me a cool feeling, knowing that I did something enriching for someone else. But the funny part about my love is if someone comes to my home and they zoom into my multiple bookcases and go "Oh my gosh, you have this book or that book", and the next thing you know, they are asking if they can borrow one of my books. Of course, it is usually one for which I have only one copy. In the early years, I'd say "sure no problem". But after many years of people not returning my little treasures, I took the next step and write in the book "Property of Debra Faris PLEASE RETURN!". Not that it actually helps get the books back. At least they can remember who put them on their amazing new path.

Gratefully, karma decided to return some little treasures. In a strange and quirky coincidence, I had three different friends say: "I

127

know you love books and I found this book and it reminded me of you. The first was literally a little red book, entitled *Little Red Book-of Sales Answers*. LoL. Another was the *Little Gold Book-of Yes Attitude*. Last but not least, I was given the coveted *Little Black Book of Connections*. What made the story even more fun was that many years later, I was at an event and didn't even know that one of the guest speakers was Jeff Gitomer. Yes, you guessed it, the one and only the author of the little red, little gold & little black books. There were no disappointments that day, besides being brilliant he was funny and charming.

Consider adding him to your influencer list.

Market like an Icon

Nike. Speedo. Coke. McDonald's. Nordstrom. Guess.

What do all of these names have in common? They're brands we recognize without any explanation. We know what they are, what they represent, and how to use them.

Developing your profile on LinkedIn is a form of branding. You're telling people who you are, what you represent, and how to use you in the future. Getting your brand across correctly is an important step. Finding the right words to communicate the right message is critical to your success.

Here's an example of branding from the banking business. Let's say someone has been successful in the home loan business. Now she wants to become a business developer so she introduces herself this way, "Hi! My name is Nancy, I used to work for Bank of America doing home loans, but what I really want to do is to work with Chase as a business developer."

What is the one thing that people will remember about her? That she is in home loans. Don't tell people what you don't want them to remember. Craft your statement very carefully to remove what you don't want and emphasize what you do want, in this case a position with Chase.

In your LinkedIn profile, tie the job description you want to everything in your profile. You may ask, "How do I make my future self into who I am now?"

It's not that hard, but it takes some thinking. You must ask the right questions to get the right answers. You tell people that you are seeking a position in whatever it is you want to do even though a lot of people say that you shouldn't do that. If you are looking for a position, you need to talk to people who know where the open positions are. You need to work on how you present your need. You may say that you "aspire for a position in...." which doesn't say you are a job seeker.

Furthermore, you need to remember that what you have done in the past has brought you to where you are today. List the places where you have volunteered and the places you have worked for. Be sure to include what you desire in all of your explanations. Tie your past into your future. This will brand you for what you want to become so people will think of you when they see the open position you are seeking.

What the mind of man can conceive and believe, the mind of man can achieve.
--Napoleon Hill

Credibility through Celebrity

Reality television shows are popular because they show how ordinary people can establish credibility through celebrity. It is a silent recommendation. If you are connected with celebrities, you must be a celebrity yourself. This is why you see so many celebrity product endorsements. It's tribal communication, meaning no words are exchanged. If a person you respect and admire likes a product or person, that product or person must be good. Why else would the celebrity endorse it?

The key point is that when you associate in any way with celebrities, you become more attractive to your peers and to potential employers. At first you may know only local celebrities. They may lead you to other even more influential celebrities like business leaders, who can ease your way into the job market. Here are three examples of how persons who started out as non-celebrities used connections with celebrities become more credible and even become celebrities themselves. It's a great demonstration of credibility through celebrity.

Following

Influencers

Richard Branson
Founder at Virgin...
✓ Following

Jack Welch
Executive Chairman,...
✓ Following

Deepak Chopra MD {...
Founder, Chopra...
✓ Following

Bill Gates
Co-chair, Bill &...
✓ Following

Arianna Huffington
President and...
✓ Following

Jeff Weiner
CEO at LinkedIn
✓ Following

James Caan
Serial Entrepreneur...
✓ Following

Gretchen Rubin
Bestselling author;...
✓ Following

Anthony (Tony) Robbi...
Chairman at Anthony...
✓ Following

Tim Brown
CEO at IDEO
✓ Following

T. Boone Pickens
Founder, Chairman...
✓ Following

Daniel Goleman
Author of FOCUS:...
✓ Following

Guy Kawasaki
Advisor at Motorola...
✓ Following

Meg Whitman
CEO at...
✓ Following

Mark Cuban
President
✓ Following

Lou Adler
CEO, best-selling...
✓ Following

Twenty years ago, I met Jay Bennett, a home business coach and mentor and a trainer for multi-level marketers, through a network marketing company, Quorum, which was owned by Raymond Hung, one of the wealthiest entrepreneurs in Hong Kong. Jay worked in many Multi-Level Marketing companies, starting with Herbalife. Network Marketing companies have always attracted personal development and leadership people; and it's always been part of their coaching and training to get new distributors.

Jay taught me that it is easier to promote someone else than to promote yourself; just like it's easier to take photos of your friends than to shoot "selfies." If you have not yet made a million dollars, it makes no sense to promote yourself as a coach who can create millionaires. However, if you associate yourself with millionaires by getting yourself photographed with them, taking courses from them, or getting into masterminds with them, people will listen to you.

You will have many opportunities to meet and associate with millionaires. Celebrities tend to become role models for society. People accept what they see from celebrities, in many cases without verifying whether the information they hear is true or not. Having a celebrity brag about you and tell others how great you are will make your job search easier. If one of the people in your network is a celebrity and they decide to promote you, think of how much that helps you in your quest!

I shared in the chapter on networking a new connection who is not only my mentor but my friend. Another way to meet celebrities is through your friends who may be connected with celebrities. I've been to several dinner parties this new connection has hosted and met several celebrities there.

One of my favorite celebrities from those dinner parties is Glenn Morshower, best known for playing Secret Service Agent Aaron Pierce in 24. He has also been in *The Transformers* and *Grizzly Park*, always playing the colonel or the tough guy. It is fascinating to me that actors can shift easily into film roles even though in reality they are nothing like the characters they play. Glenn is the farthest thing from being a tough guy. He is a very funny man, with a memory like a fox.

He started out like everyone else, completely unknown. In his early days at auditions, he would go out for parts and not get them. He would study and work, but success eluded him. Then one day he put syrup in his shoes and he got the part. "Hmm," he thought, "Let's try something else." Next he put cornflakes in his shoes and got the part. His wife was always part of his scheme and helped fill his shoes to insure he would get the part. Since his schemes were working, every time he auditioned he would create a ridiculous scheme to anchor himself. These games gave him the self-confidence he needed to start getting parts and build his own celebrity.

Luck is what happens when preparation meets opportunity.
--Seneca

One of today's most recognized seminar speakers is James Malinchak, famous for being on the *Secret Millionaire* television show. He trademarks himself as a Big Money speaker, and has created his *Big Money Speaker Boot Camp*, and his *College Speaker Success Boot Camp*. In both events, he develops and trains entrepreneurs to speak, coach, and build or improve their businesses. James is known for his philanthropic charitable gifts. In the *Secret Millionaire*, James helped three families get back on their feet with generous donations.

However, James was not always a celebrity. I remember him years ago speaking on small seminar stages to build his reputation. Unlike most of these speakers, James knew that to build celebrity, he needed to associate with celebrities. In the beginning, such opportunities were rare but he took advantage of every one. It only takes a single connection to open the door and for James one connection led to many more.

Now he brings many celebrities he has met over the years to his events to share their message with the speakers and entrepreneurs in the audience.

One of my favorite celebrity speakers is Les Brown, whose events I've attended for over 20 years. He is often a guest speaker at Malinchak's events and the crowds love him. On the sports side, I enjoy hearing James' good friend Joe Theismann, a former National Football League quarterback. Theismann is the subject of several highly popular sports videos on YouTube showing the tragic, career-ending football injury he suffered in 1985. He teaches audiences that even after game changing events, you can turn your life into a huge success. James connects celebrities with his audiences and teaches them how to gain credibility by increasing their own celebrity connections. By using his celebrity connections, James Malinchak also gives his own event credibility.

You can give yourself credibility by finding and connecting with celebrities in the field you want to enter. They are not hard to find or meet if you position yourself correctly.

People Also Viewed

When you were a little kid did anyone ever tell you a fish story? My dad actually told me once we were going on a snipe hunt. We had to wait until the sun went down and it was dark. We had to be quiet and were searching for snipes with a flashlight. We put our shoes on grabbed our flashlights and pillow cases and headed out into the night to catch our snipes.

Lo and behold, my father had me outside calling for snipe but all I heard was a cricket. After 30 minutes my dad said there must not be any snipes out tonight and we came in. Later that summer he took me fishing. He gave me a fishing pole, taught me how to bait the hook and propped me up on a quaint little bridge. Then he tromped off in his golf shoes to shoot nine holes of golf. When he returned, I told him I had caught three fish. He shook his head. What happened was I did catch one fish but when I pulled him up and he hit the ground, a small fish popped out of this first fish and an even smaller fish came out.

People Also Viewed

Katishia Cosley Trigg
Show Host at KTRK, Live Well Network

Ellie Scarborough Brett
founder at Media Bombshell

Lauren Freeman
Anchor at KPRC-TV

Kym Forester
Membership Director at National
Insurance Crime Bureau

Anjuli Lohn
Reporter at FOX 13 WTVT-TV

Katie McCall
Reporter & Fill-in Anchor at Fox 26
Houston

Deborah Bussell
Business Development Manager at The
Next Up

Annie Velasquez
Otter Relations Business Partner at
OtterBox

Sarah Cole
Licensed Realtor at Harcourts Prime
Properties

Dominique Sachse
News Anchor at KPRC-TV

Shared stories are bridge builders. This is one of my top 20 favorite functions on LinkedIn. On LinkedIn, when you as a viewer look at a person's profile, it shows you other people that that this person's viewers also viewed. For example, if you look up Oprah Winfrey, it may show you other talk show hosts that people also viewed. My favorite story of "Who knows Who" goes back to when I received an invite from the most successful real estate coach in the United States, CEO and real estate coach Mike Ferry™. When I looked at his profile, I noticed that people also viewed Floyd Wickman and when I clicked on Floyd I saw that people viewed

Tommy Hopkins and when I viewed Tommy I saw people viewed Brian Tracy and when I clicked on Brian I saw that people viewed Tony Robbins and that put the biggest smile on my face because Tony was one of my mentors. :) When you use the "People Also Viewed" feature on LinkedIn, you identify people that you may not know but may need in your job search. Look at the "People Also Viewed" feature when doing research on LinkedIn and you may find some valuable connections.

Who knows Who

While viewing the profiles of potential recruiters, you may see something you like, maybe one of their second-level connections or someone who gave them a recommendation, someone they recommended, or maybe someone who endorsed them. You realize that you too want to connect with that person. When you click on that person's name or picture to look at their profile, it creates a path for spiders, the bits of software that track all LinkedIn activity. At the end of the day those paths are added up and you become part of the list of people who most viewed that person's profile. This is important because it is part of the social proof that begins with ripples, becomes rivers, and leads to tribes in this arena of online presence. Most of us are curious about who likes whom or who follows whom because in the job-searching world, that person may be the one who is one or two degrees or levels away from introducing us to our dream job. This applies to any activity, including hobbies, romance, and recreation.

Keep in Touch Marketing

In the Real Estate industry, a common practice is to send out a monthly newsletter. In other industries, companies send holiday postcards on special occasions every month, including Valentine's Day, Easter, St. Patrick's Day, Christmas, and Thanksgiving. All these cards include a special message advertising the company's service or specials.

Even the owner of a small business starting out on a shoestring budget from his kitchen table can do this. This business owner will use Vistaprint to get his first set of business cards at a reasonable price. The next step for him is to print advertising postcards with photos of dogs wearing silly hats, cats dressed up in costumes, and even bearded dragons wearing dresses. Why? So he can make his business memorable.

This works on LinkedIn as well. Wouldn't it be cool if you updated your friends and family at the Holidays with not just a photo of your newest outfit but a real update? Share your events with "Photo Marketing" cards. Then, six months later, you can do even more updates. If you know the companies you're interested in working with, you can send the contacts from those companies your LinkedIn Profile.

Who did they recommend & who recommended them?

In the banking and loan business, a lender will ask for two years of tax returns or six months of previous utility bills to verify that payments were made in the manner necessary to grant the credit on a loan.

In the world of LinkedIn, when it comes to verifying a person's depth of experience, nothing speaks louder than recommendations from former colleagues and bosses. Using your network to build up strong recommendations is an important piece of the LinkedIn puzzle. When a potential employer sees a recommendation on your profile, it gives your resume extra validation and verification.

On the other hand, who have you recommended? Are you giving endorsements to the right individuals for the right reasons? When employers see who you have endorsed and recommended, they may also use this information in their decision-making process.

Recommendations

Networking & LinkedIn Coach
The Chief Networking Officer

Andrea L. Russo
I am your ambassador of first impressions actively seeking a career position working with Seniors in my local area

" Debra recently spoke at my church where I was a former "Hospitality Coordinator" there with Career Renewal Ministries. She was truly amazing! She shared personal stories that were so empowering and motivating. Her knowledge and expertise with navigating through the proper usage and getting the most out of your LinkedIn page proved to be invaluable to me. Thank you again... **more**

January 16, 2014, Andrea L. worked directly with Debra at The Chief Networking Officer

★Batista Gremaud★
Body Design Formula Leadership Team Builder and Visionuary ◆ Author ◆

" Debra Farris is most qualified and knowledgeable in the LinkedIn applications. She has helped me personally create an appealing profile and has shared with me some very valuable strategies. I recommend her to anyone who wants to use LinkedIn to accelerate their business growth and amplify their social media presence.
Batista Gremaud
Body Design Formula - Dr Fitness USA

January 31, 2013, ★Batista was with another company when working with Debra at The Chief Networking Officer

Patti Langell
Contributor at Hollywood52.com | Social Media Consultant | Social Entrepreneur

" I have taken many courses on using LinkedIn and I felt confident that I was more knowledgeable than most on the best practices for using it. Then I met Debra Faris and took a LinkedIn course from her. All I can say is wow! She showed me things I know most LinkedIn trainers don't even know how to do. It takes a lot to impress me since I have been around social media for a... **more**

January 9, 2013, Patti was Debra's client

Testimonials are your best friend

The biggest question I get concerns my opinion on swapping recommendations. I admit that at first I didn't like the idea but when I thought about it, it seemed logical in certain situations.

Let's say I invested a lot of time coaching a client and gave them a tip that made them a very substantial amount of money and then realized that they had mentored me years before through a book they wrote that helped hundreds, thousands, or millions of people, including myself. I would want a recommendation from that person for the work I did and would not hesitate to give them one knowing the value of the services he had performed for me.

My answer to that question is simple. Was value exchanged? I won't write a general recommendation for you nor expect one from you if nothing of value happened. I would only recommend you if I personally experienced your value and can in good conscience stand behind the recommendation. Back in Chapter 1, "Who Am I," I showed you that if you were a Boy or Girl Scout and your scoutmaster had known you for years and knew your character well, they would definitely stand behind their recommendation. The best recommendations come from people with the integrity to give an unequivocal positive recommendation.

Be a producer using iPhone Videos

For every force, there is a counter force, for every negative there is a positive, for every action there is a reaction. For every cause, there is an effect.
--Grace Speare

Have you ever used your cell phone to look up a YouTube video and then shared it with your friends because it meant something or was funny? By encouraging users to post videos and photos on the site, LinkedIn has made it easier for us to use technology to bring us to life for the world to see just like people on the big screen and on reality television. Make your profile more eye-catching by adding video. People love to watch movies, television, and YouTube. Let them watch a video of you!

LinkedIn has made it easier. Since we use our cell phones for everything now, including pictures and videos, we can make high quality visual presentations that make us all look professional on LinkedIn.

Here are This Chapter's Business Consultant Influencers

As you read these profiles, look for possible referrals for your needs.

Is there something in their story you connect with?
C9ould you gain a new idea or insight for your business or career?
Who do you know or who do they know that can help both of you?
If you needed help or wanted to buy a product, what would it be?
How do you follow up when you meet someone?
When people view your profile, how do you want them to feel?
Do your tribes line up so you could be Power Partners?
What are your favorite questions to ask in an introductory call?

Look deep into nature, and then you will understand everything better.
~ Albert Einstein

I first discovered the principle of "adding value first" when my brother and I set up a roadside pecan stand near our home. But business was slow. The owner of the orchard where we got our pecans, instead of being mad, offered a large bowl of shelled pecans and said, "you'll attract more people if you offer a sample." We did and people stopped to sample the nuts and our sales soared.

Today, I work with socially conscious entrepreneurs and business people from all walks of life that have something to share with the world. Together, we develop successful marketing campaigns that foster the growth of customer communities through adding consistent up-front value that generates trust, loyalty and continuity.

▶ Develop the perfect marketing strategy and funnel for your product or service.

▶ Tailor your message and up-front value proposition to attract your core customer.

▶ Create trust, affinity and community around your brand and watch your business grow.

Specialties: ★ Automation / InfusionSoft / Marketing Strategies & Tactics / Traffic & Conversions ★ Content Development / Funnel Development / Joint Venture Development ★ Email Marketing / Marketing Campaigns / Webinar Scripting / Email Scripting ★ Customer Retention / Landing Page Development / Paid Traffic ★

What three books do you feel are a must that you highly recommend others to read? Psycho-Cybernetics, Influence: The Psychology of Persuasion, Think and Grow Rich.

What movie touched you by its meaning or inspired you? Rudy

Who in your childhood was a major influence that helped shape your life? My Grandpa

Who now is a Mentor, Coach or Strategist that is on your advisory council? Mike Assum

If you could be anyone for a day, who would it be and what experience can you envision? Richard Branson, experience talking and helping change makers all day while having fun on an island

What discipline could someone learn from you: Having a Power Team

What subject or argument most stirs your emotions, why? Psychology

When "winning someone over" do you think facts or emotions carry the day? Emotions. Then mind confirms what the heart wants.

What do you wish you spent more time doing? What prevents you from doing that now? Nothing

In helping others, is it better to teach them, give them, or show them? Show them

Aaron's Favorite Characteristics

Accountable / Disciplined / Efficient / Honorable / Innovative / Reliable / Resourceful

Aaron Watson "Mr. Monetization"
Value Grows & Money Flows Where Evergrowth Goes
▶ 505-321-1754 ▶ Aaron@Evergrowth.co www.Evergrowth.co

Ann DeVere

**Executive Producer AccessToExperts.TV,
Meet The Press LIVE,
Turn Your SHOW Into CA$H,
TurnYourInterviewsIntoCASH.com**

You don't have to be a Star to star in your own TV show – Ann DeVere

It's 2005 and it's a lovely spring afternoon in beautiful San Diego, California. I'm in my office. The phone rings and I hear "Oh Ann, I just have to share this. Yesterday I was watching a show on money management. While the information she shared would help most people, it would be devastating for a lot of others and they don't even know that. I just have to get on TV and share this information Now!" This was one of those pivotal moments for me!

Today I help Experts expand their Global Visibility so they can be seen and heard by the people who need their help.

► Speakers, Authors, Coaches: How would you like to leverage the full power of WebTV by turning your Expertise into your own WebTV show on Facebook LIVE or any other WebTV platform?

► Go-Global: How would you like to broadcast your show from your own Home Studio that you can easily set up for a few hundred dollars?

► Experts: Learn to Ask questions like a TV Reporter, Voice your opinion like a TV Journalist, Interview your guests like your favorite Show Hosts on TV!

SPECIALTIES: I'm a Speaker, Consultant and Media Trainer. Our online & in person experiential training programs include "Turn Your Show Into Cash", "Turn Your Interviews Into CASH" and "Lights, Camera, Interview!!!"

I've merged my full service international business consulting firm with my husband, Michael DeVere, and with his 30 years of experience in TV: from directing the 6 o'clock news, to working on productions for HBO, The History Channel, CBS, NBC, ABC, ESPN, Nickelodeon, MTV, Comedy Central, National Geographic, and more.

What one books do you feel are a must that you highly recommend others to read? The Greatest Miracle in the World "Og Mandino"

What movie touched you by its meaning or inspired you? It's a Wonderful Life

What will you do differently this year from last year or what do you want more of? Opening my tour of the GlobalVisibility Initiative beginning in the USA, Europe, Australia, Asia

Who now is a Mentor, Coach or Strategist that is on your advisory council? Dame DC Cordova her Love for Excellerated Business Growth

If you could have any superpower (or be any superhero), what/who would it be and why? Have everyone see themselves through God's eyes so they can know how powerful, gifted and amazing they are.

In helping others, is it better to teach them, give them, or show them? Teach them. "Teach them to fish, feed them for life!"

If there were one problem in the world you could solve, what would it be? Uncompassionate people

Ann's Favorite Characteristics

Brilliant, Intuitive, Visionary, Strategic, Empowering, Compassionate

Ann DeVere aka *"The Global Visibility Catalyst"* "Meet The Press LIVE"
& "The Global Visibility Initiative"
TV Show for Every Expert, No Expert Left Behind".
Executive Producer of "Access To Experts TV", Speaker & Consultant
▶www.TurnYouShowIntoCASH.com ◀▶ mail@GVNTV.com ◀
▶619-302-7952◀

Marketing is a contest for people's attention. `Seth Godin

At the age of nine my creative brain was already drawing pictures of cars and buildings, and I enjoyed inventing my own designs. I was so in love with cars that I saved up the money to purchase a red 1932 Plymouth before I even got my drivers license, and I still continue to work on and drive it! That's where I learned the importance of finding solutions to a problem, setting measurable goals and the joy of reaping the benefits.

Today, I own my own Marketing/PR agency and work with a diversity of size businesses all over the United States with a team of professionals. We've been able to help one client get on the Food Network, an RV Manufacturer featured on the front page of USA Today and also ABC World News with Diane Sawyer. in the Western U.S. with Outdoor, TV, and Print media, and we succeeded.

▶ **Get Media Coverage for Your Business**. It's more believable when your prospects read an article or story about your company or you.

▶ **Be Seen as The Leader in Your Industry and Not a Follower.** People like working with winners. Be seen by your prospects as an Innovator and someone who everyone wants to work with.

▶ **Implement a Marketing Strategy to Meet and Exceed Your Goals**. We create a Manageable, Measurable and Achievable Marketing Process for our clients.

Specialties: Auto, Food and Sporting Goods Branding / Auto, Food and Sporting Goods Marketing / Bottom Line Growth / Publicity / PR / Media Exposure / Advertising Campaigns / Social Media Management / Websites / Designing Packages/Sales Materials

Who in your childhood was a major influence that helped shape your life? My dad. After 20+ years working for a company (McDonnell Douglas), he decided to start his own business. It was at our family business that my brother and I learned how to work with customers and how to run a small business.

What will you do differently this year from last year or what do you want more of? I want to continue working with business entrepreneurs showing them how to plan for success and how to reach their goals.

If you could be anyone for a day, who would it be and what experience can you envision? Steve Jobs. His had the ability to be a visionary and know how to create new markets that will improve our lives.

What discipline could someone learn from you? How to listen to a person when they are speaking and not interrupt them or begin thinking what you want to say before the speaker is finished.

When "winning someone over" do you think facts or emotions carry the day? Facts help support a particular side to an argument, but emotions will win over the facts.

In helping others, is it better to teach them, give them, or show them? I believe teaching someone is better because it will make those you teach remember what is taught.

If there were one problem in the world you could solve, what would it be? Respect. If we could learn to respect others, we can become better humans.

George's Favorite Characteristics
Creative, Punctual, "Left Brain & Right Brain", Serving Others

George Carson aka "Thoughts to Conception"
"We Make Great Things Happen in Your Marketing and Brand Awareness"
♛ Brand Awareness ♛ Marketing Problem Solvers ♛
Core Branding ♛ PR
♜ gcarson@CarsonMarketingInc.com ♟ 949-477-9400 ♛
www.CarsonMarketingInc.com

The older I get the less I listen
to what people say

and the more I look
at what they do.

Andrew Carnegie

Chapter 9
Jobs, Industries, and Culture

I found that luck is quite predictable. If you want more luck, take more chances. Be more active. Show up more often.

--Brian Tracy

Brian Tracy
I Help Business Owners and Entrepreneurs Achieve Their Personal And Business Goals Faster

Greater San Diego Area | Professional Training & Coaching

Current	Brian Tracy International
Previous	5 Hour Energy
Education	University of Alberta

Connect ▼

500+
connections

My Influencers: Brian Tracy

One of the fun things I learned about LinkedIn is that you can look at "People also View," where members leave a trail. One of my first coaches was Mike Ferry. When I viewed his profile, I noticed that people who viewed him also viewed Floyd Wickman, which led me to Tommy Hopkins, then to Brian Tracy, and then to Tony Robbins, another mentor of mine. I mention this again because it is a perfect example of a trajectory, a path that leads to successful people. It is important that you look for leaders and experts in your field, because this will be one of your gold mines or "Ahas" on LinkedIn.

Brian Tracy is a business trainer who has coached and consulted to over 1,000 companies and spoken to over 5,000,000 people in talks and seminars around the world on topics such as Entrepreneurial Success, Million Dollar Habits, Psychology of Selling, Science of Self-Confidence, Goal Setting, and Time Management. He is best-selling

147

author of over 45 books that have been translated into dozens of languages.

At the beginning of my career, I found myself needing to learn more than I knew. First I learned the necessary skills in the education process, but I also knew I needed the other side, people skills. I need more than the "Hi, how are you?" kind of networking so many people use. I needed to learn real people skills, including the laws of success and psychology, then cross the bridge into the relationship building skills.

When choosing between two similar applicants, hiring managers are increasingly turning to social media outlets to supplement information they are unable to glean from applications or interviews.
--Amy Jo Martin

When I met Brian Tracy, I was learning sales during a time when most people thought of "salesman and salesperson" as bad words. They saw a "salesperson" as someone who wanted to sell them something they didn't want. The truth is we all buy things every day and, from the time we were little kids, we were selling our parents on them buying or giving us whatever we wanted. Sales psychology is part human psychology that studies why we do or want things. Sales is the art of satisfying the demand for products and services when and where they are needed.

Abraham Maslow, in "Maslow's Law," showed us that all humans have a hierarchy of basic needs. First we search for safety, then shelter, then water, then food. When we meet someone new, we follow a similar hierarchy. First we need to get to know them, then to like them, and then to trust them. As we go through this process, they get to know us, like us, and trust us. This is part of the process of "following up and following through" with everybody we meet. When we do this consistently, we create strong people skills and habits.

> *"Successful people are simply those with successful habits."* Brian Tracy

Do you remember the movie *The Secret*? It is all about the "Law of Attraction." One of my mentors, Dr. John Demartini, who was in *The Secret,* shared with me that the law of attraction is only one of many universal laws. At that time, I used to have a university on wheels (my car) where I listen to Brian Tracy's audio program, "The Universal Laws of Success and Achievement," in which he talked about more than 100 universal laws. Using such programs to understand the psychology of selling and to build self-confidence is a critical part of the ongoing learning process in our lives.

When you listen to audios in your car or watch late night YouTube videos late at night, you expand your awareness how communication with others helps them and helps us achieve our goals. This is a fundamental part of your personal development and your personal growth.

Consider adding him to your influencer list.

You are more than your resume

Names, dates, employers, job description. Is this how you want someone to judge you as a person? You are much than your resume. Do you manage others? Are you involved in execution, project management, or time management? Are you involved in charities? Do you have personal hobbies that you enjoy? You are more than a two-dimensional piece of paper with your work history listed on it. In many cases, potential employers use your resume to make decisions on who gets the interview and who gets the job. If you show up as a well-rounded person with interests and passions outside work, you are much more likely to get in the door.

Talent alone won't make you a success. Neither will being in the right place at the right time, unless you are ready. The most important question

is: "Are you ready?"
--Johnny Carson

As you use LinkedIn and continue your career and personal thread, as we started to do in the "Who am I" chapter, you realize you are so much more than your resume. The most important question becomes, "How do you match yourself with your new LinkedIn friends from all areas of your life?" Building an effective profile, making strong connections, and connecting with the right influencers can give people much more insight into who *you* are as a person, both at work and at home. As more and more recruiters and employers use LinkedIn for recruiting purposes, a good profile will put you light years ahead of potential employees who include only work-related information on their profile.

The Difference Between Recruiters, Headhunters & Outplacements

Recruiters, headhunters, and human resources directors are all very important people to you in your quest for the right job. How do you find them on LinkedIn? Start with a LinkedIn search for people who use these titles in their descriptions. You will quickly identify the appropriate people for your industry. Connect with them and begin to develop a relationship with them. Connect to as many as you want. Then start to build rapport, find out what they're looking for in the perfect candidate, and examine their profile. Do your research, build a great relationship, and set yourself up for the perfect job.

Many groups on LinkedIn, if used effectively, can be instrumental in helping you find and land your dream job. Search and connect to groups in your chosen industry and then connect to the people in those groups. These connections will become extremely valuable as you look for interviews, recommendations, and networking.

"The primary reason for failure is that people do not develop new plans to replace those plans that didn't work." ---**Napoleon Hill**

Here's a bonus. I'm sharing my recruiter list of super-connectors with you. Each of these recruiters is connected to thousands of employers and can assist you in connecting the right employer for your field.

Top 12 Big Connectors - Recruiters & HR

Stacy (Berman) Birnbach | 25,000+ connections
1st

CEO/President Verus

Washington D.C. Metro Area | Staffing and Recruiting

Current	The Leukemia & Lymphoma Society, Verus Consulting Solutions, Verus Staffing Solutions
Previous	Health Search International and Clinical Resources, Health Search International, Clinical Resources Inc.
Education	University of Maryland

Send a message | Endorse ▾

500+
connections

Patrick Campbell
1st

Talent Acquisition Consultant at Public Storage

Greater Los Angeles Area | Staffing and Recruiting

Current	Public Storage
Previous	Union Bank [through Collabrus], TIAA-CREF through Pride Staffing, Campbell Executive Services, Inc.
Education	Ferris State University

Send a message | Endorse ▾

500+
connections

Derrick Coshow ★ Top Linked™ 21,000+
1st

Lead Technical Recruiter at Accolo

Las Vegas, Nevada Area | Staffing and Recruiting

Previous	Aristocrat, Link Technologies, Caesars Entertainment Corporation
Education	University of Nevada-Las Vegas

Send a message | Endorse ▾

500+
connections

Eric Grenier

2nd

30,104+ direct connections "Top 10 Most Connected"
follow me on twitter: @comcentric

Greater Denver Area | Information Technology and Services

Current	Comcentric Inc.
Previous	RSA Companies, Profitool Inc., MW Builders / MMC Corporation
Education	University of Colorado at Denver

Connect | Send Eric InMail ▼

500+
connections

Bill Gunn

1st

G&A Principal | Build Your Talent Brand | Select the
Exceptional from the Best | 23,315 Direct Connections
Top 1% Viewed

Charlotte, North Carolina Area | Management Consulting

Current	G&A
Previous	Unisys, CSC, Mitsui & Co., Ltd.
Education	Old Dominion University

Send a message | Endorse ▼

500+
connections

Varsha Karnad - linkedin.varsha@gmail.com -Netwrk-22000+

1st

Executive – Human Resources at Kraft Foods

Mumbai Area, India | Human Resources

Current	Kraft Foods - Cadbury India Ltd
Previous	Indira School Of Business Studies, ISBS – Pune, Think People Solutions Pvt Ltd
Education	Indira School Of Business Studies - ISBS

Send a message | Endorse ▼

500+
connections

Ann Zaslow-Rethaber

1st

President at International Search Consultants AIRS
Diversity Certified Recruiter

Phoenix, Arizona Area | Staffing and Recruiting

Current	International Search Consultants, Inc.
Previous	Owigi Films
Education	AIRS Diversity Certified Recruiter

Send a message | Endorse ▼

500+
connections

Leonie Sands Mrep CertRP {LION 20,000+}

1st

Recruitment Consultant at Aptus Life Science

Exeter, United Kingdom | Staffing and Recruiting

Previous   Spinnaker Contract Services Limited, The Hammond Recruitment Group Ltd, Storm Recruitment

Education   University of Westminster

Send a message   Endorse   ▼

500+
connections

Pete Tzavalas 1,000+(LION)

1st

Sr. Vice President at Challenger, Gray & Christmas, Inc.

petetzavalas@challengergray.com 818.536.1415

Greater Los Angeles Area | Human Resources

Current   Challenger, Gray & Christmas, Inc.

Previous   Robert Half International, Right Management, Brinks Home Security

Education Biola University

Send a message   Endorse   ▼

500+
connections

Scott Simon

1st

BetterHire Provider/Consultant 29.999 connections

Birmingham, Alabama Area | Staffing and Recruiting

Current   Betterhire.com Provider/Consulting, TechnologyAlabama.com, Access Points

Previous   Adatech Inc., National Life, National Life Group

Education University of Alabama at Birmingham

Send a message   Endorse   ▼

500+
connections

Phil Rosenberg

LinkedIn's most connected Career Coach (30K+ 31M+),
Author http://reCareered.com, Top 20 on Linkedin globally

Greater Denver Area | Human Resources

Current	reCareered, Business Week, PersonalBranding Blog, TheLadders, CIO, Fast Company, Career Central group on Linkedin
Previous	Robert Half Management Resources, Robert Half Technology, New Horizons Computer Learning Centers
Education	Northwestern University - Kellogg School of Management

Send a message   Endorse   ▼

500+
connections

Tom Toole

1st

One of the Management Recruiter's Most Connected
Recruiters bringing "Midwest Work Ethic" to his Clients.
20k+ 1st LION

Orange County, California Area | Staffing and Recruiting

Current	Management Recruiters International/MRINetwork, Management Recruiter's International - Southern Ca.- National Market
Previous	The Coca-Cola Company, Wisconsin Air National Guard(USAF)-128th ARW, Caterpillar
Education	Marquette University

Send a message   Endorse   ▼

500+
connections

Websites are Your Research Tool

When you're interested in working for a company, you need to do your homework and research the company. Ask yourself why you would want to work for them. Take another look at the job description, review their website, and look for current events on the web. A job description tells you not just about the position you want but also gives you the voice of the company. See if their values align with yours. Check into their history, their ideals, their expectations, and investigate everything you can about the company and its hiring manager.

You can also connect with company insiders to get a sense of the corporate culture. If you are researching a public company, you can check quarterly and annual financial reports to get a feel for the challenges the company faces and the direction it is going.

No occupation is so delightful to me as the culture of the earth, and no culture comparable to that of the garden.

--Thomas Jefferson

Create a file for that company and add all the material that you find. Put the link to the company website in your file, create a list of key job titles, find the incumbents by searching on LinkedIn, add them to the list, review their profiles and invite them to connect. Your knowledge of your potential employer will make your interview more effective and will better equip you to understand whether the job fits your potential new career. Think of it as buying a textbook, highlighting the important lessons, identifying the takeaways, and using what you learned.

News

Leadership & Manag...
4,448,110 followers
✓ Following

Big Ideas & Innovation
3,734,135 followers
✓ Following

Technology
3,189,912 followers
✓ Following

Entrepreneurship & ...
2,826,271 followers
✓ Following

Marketing Strategies
2,723,532 followers
✓ Following

Social Media
2,341,889 followers
✓ Following

Professional Women
2,252,170 followers
✓ Following

Economy
1,905,200 followers
✓ Following

Best Advice
1,395,840 followers
✓ Following

Education
1,341,732 followers
✓ Following

Healthcare
1,244,852 followers
✓ Following

Recruiting & Hiring
1,137,566 followers
✓ Following

Positions vs. Industries

Are you searching for a position or do you want to be part of the industry? Using LinkedIn and managing your connections correctly can set you up for either. If you want to work in a given industry, connect with successful people in that industry and influencers who reflect the industry, and then network with people currently working in the industry. If you seek a position, highlight your skills, connect with leaders and mentors who can assist you in achieving your goals, and gain the recommendations needed from leaders in your field.

Let's look at a few specific industries to give you a better idea. In the banking industry, for instance, the following might come to mind when you think of banking: branch manager, teller, loan officer, commercial banking, investment banking, financial services and management, the list is endless. You can investigate, research, and entertain hundreds of positions within the banking industry. Once you identify your ideal banking position, highlight your skills, and connect to the right team.

Another avenue for many is the retail industry, which is always looking for great candidates. If you don't want to work in sales, look into the corporate part of retail, including buyers, operations managers, human resources, regional managers, training departments, again the list of opportunities is endless. Search by the position you seek and begin to interact with the people who can help get you there.

The entertainment industry is also huge. Are you a performer looking to be on movie screens in front of millions of fans, a singer with fans following your concerts across the country, or do you want to act on the Broadway stage? If performing does not interest you but you want to work in the entertainment industry, you can become a director, key grip, special effects person, design costumes, be a makeup artist, or become an executive assistant, screenwriter, caterer, or one of the many thousands of people that support the team on stage. Find the industry and position you want, and then use your connections on LinkedIn to build the relationships needed to get that job.

Culture is the process by which a person becomes all that they were created capable of being.
--Thomas Carlyle

To go deeper, if you see yourself as a leader climbing the corporate ladder, you may wonder, "How can I find that path?" Success does leave a trail and with LinkedIn you can see how mentors carve a path you can follow.

LinkedIn gives you the opportunity to see other people's success trails. On a CFO'S profile, you can see how he ended up in his current position by following his story on LinkedIn back 10, 12, or 15 years to where he or she started, perhaps as an accountant, then as a Certified Public Accountant (CPA) then controller and finally Chief Financial Officer (CFO).

Think International

Are you fluent in Spanish, Italian, Farsi, Cantonese, or German? Is your primary language something other than English? Back when I was in the loan business, I led a mastermind group for a Keller Williams Real Estate office. Acquiring new business was a key challenge. I asked a group of 10 real estate agents I knew, four of whom were Hispanic, three Chinese, one Cantonese, one Persian and one Polish, "Were any of you actually born in another country?" Half of them were. Then I asked, "Do you have family in another country?" Most of them had relatives overseas. I asked them whether there were any commonalities in their last names. The girl from Poland said, "Yes, Polish names end in 'ski." I asked the title company if they could do a search by origin of names and they said yes. So we began to hunt.

International Groups on LinkedIn

Organization	Members
Amnesty Intl (protect Human rights worldwide)	30,000
ASIS International	59,000
BNI - Business Network International	33,000
Builders, Owners, & managers International	43,300
IFMA International Facility Management Association	28,000
IIBA International Institute of Business Analysis	60,000
International Assn of Business communicators	32,000
International baccalaureate	25,000
International Business	71,000
International Coast Fed (Sustainable Development)	40,000
International Council of Shopping Centers	39,000
International Freight	28,000
International Import/Export	129,000
International Network for the Arts (Theater and art)	23,000
International Relations Professionals	30,000
International relations/Affairs	30,000
International School Educators	21,000
International Society for Technology/Education	41,000
International sports	27,000
International Trade	56,000
International TV Professionals	57,000
Jobs in NGOS	27,000
Sustainable Green	30,000
Technical Assistance Consultancy Network	34,000
Toastmasters International	36,000
Zezex (International Development)	47,000

If you know 100 people who know you, like you, and trust you, you have all the connections you need. This is especially true if you speak a foreign language. A former colleague, a bank branch manager, who spoke Farsi and had the biggest book of business in Orange County, put this idea to use when she advertised for business in Los Angeles. She attracted half her clientele from Los Angeles because many of them were more comfortable speaking their native language when they did business.

One of the challenges for any retail organization is communicating with people from different backgrounds. Another friend of mine managed a home improvement store in Los Angeles located in an area where Chinese-speaking individuals lived. Very few of them shopped at his store. To change that pattern, my friend found an employee who spoke Chinese and assigned him the mission of getting his Chinese friends to shop at the store. As an added inducement, he was to be their personal shopper so they would feel comfortable when they arrived. The associate she picked was a special needs employee with a job coach. When his manager put him on his new task as Chinese Lead Generator, his eyes lit up and he was excited every time a new customer came to him for help. He became a needed individual in the store and was called on by all departments to assist in translation. It changed the way he looked at his job when he became a valued member of the team. Sales increased as more and more Chinese-speaking customers visited the store.

If you go on LinkedIn and put the word "Spanish" in the search engine and select "people," you will find over 4,546,000 names.

Polish people add 257,757, Chinese account for 1,115,000, and Italians 1,195,000. Continue your search in your native language or secondary language and you'll find thousands of individuals who share that language with you. Be sure to add all the languages you speak and your proficiency to your profile so those searching for speakers of other languages can find you easily.

If you search the word "International" on LinkedIn, you will find 19,000 results. From financial services, IT, accounting, computer software, to management consultants, people around the world are connecting to each other. You will find 46,000 international groups on LinkedIn including fashion, import and export trade, freight, television professionals, Beta Gamma Sigma honor society, and Toastmasters International. LinkedIn makes doing business on a global level easier.

The chart above shows you how many members many of the international groups on LinkedIn have.

Organizational chart: Who connects to who?

When researching a new company, one of the best things to use, if you can get it, is their organizational chart. This will show you how the company is organized and who is connected and how.

Sample Divisional Organizational Structure

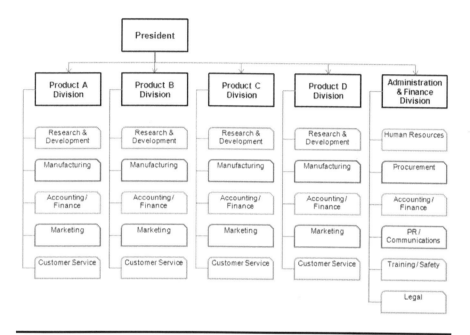

I am convinced that nothing we do is more important than hiring and developing people. At the end of the day you bet on people, not on strategies.
--Larry Bossidy

People Don't Hire Resumes, They Hire People

Whether he or she is CEO of the company or Director of HR, the hiring manager will always choose the best fit for the culture of their organization. In a research company, this could mean the best person is one who knows how to research in a creative way. In a sales position, they're looking for a relationship builder, an ambassador position, for a person with credibility. They hire you because of your character, your values, and your integrity. They hire you as a person.

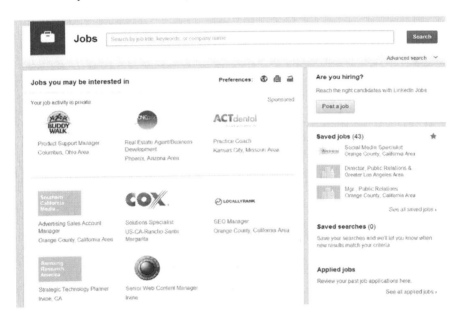

How do you effectively align yourself or find the right people that will introduce you to the right people? Here's where using LinkedIn in an effective manner can be of great benefit! Once your profile is built with authenticity and transparency, you've started building relationships and connections with your top 100 as well as their top 100's, and you've done your research on your top five companies, it will all fall into place. You will be aligned with the right people. They will know your character and potential because of the relationship you have built with them. As you research the companies and people within those companies, your network will assist you in making the connections and aligning yourself.

Working for Non-Profits

After a conversation with Jim Palmer one day, I looked on LinkedIn and discovered that over 6,000 people had Non-Profit in their profile. While looking for opportunities, do not neglect non-profit organizations. These organizations represent amazing causes and hire people with all sorts of knowledge.

Find Connections in Your Top Five Companies

If you have created your profile on LinkedIn and have done your research as I've shown you, you will be well on your way to finding that new job. As you look at companies and opportunities, begin to identify the most important people in the companies you're searching.

Industry List from LinkedIn	
Accounting	Airlines/Aviation
Alternative Dispute Resolution	Alternative Medicine
Animation	Apparel & Fashion
Architecture & Planning	Arts & Crafts
Automotive	Aviation & Aerospace
Banking	Biotechnology
Broadcast Media	Building Materials
Business Supplies, Equipment	Capital Markets
Chemicals	Civic & Social Organization
Civil Engineering	Commercial Real Estate
Computer & Network Security	Computer Games
Computer Hardware	Computer Software
Construction	Consumer Electronics
Consumer Goods	Consumer Services
Cosmetics	Dairy
Defense & Space	Design
Education Management	E-Learning
Electronic Manufacturing	Entertainment
Environmental Services	Event Services
Executive Offices	Facilities Services
Farming	Financial Services
Fine Art	Fisheries
Food & Beverages	Food Production

Fund-Raising	Furniture
Gambling & Casinos	Glass, Ceramics, & Concrete
Government Administration	Government Relations
Graphic Design	Health, Wellness & Fitness
Higher Education	Hospital & Health Care
Hospitality	Human Resources
Import & Export	Individual & Family Services
Industrial Automation	Information Services
International Affairs	Insurance
Information Technology and Services	International Trade & Development
Internet	Investment Banking
Investment Management	Judiciary
Law Enforcement	Law Practice
Legal Services	Legislative Office
Leisure, Travel, & Tourism	Libraries
Logistics & Supply Chain	Luxury Goods & Jewelry
Machinery	Management Consulting
Maritime	Marketing and Advertising
Market Research	Mechanical Engineering
Media Production	Medical Devices
Medical Practice	Mental Health Care
Military	Mining & Metals
Motion Pictures & Films	Museums & Institutions
Music	Nanotechnology
Newspapers	Nonprofit Organization Mgmt
Oil & Energy	Online Media
Outsourcing/Offshoring	Package/Freight Delivery
Packaging & Containers	Paper & Forest Products
Performing Arts	Pharmaceuticals
Philanthropy	Photography
Plastics	Political Organization
Primary/Secondary Education	Printing
Professional Trainer and Coach	Program Development
Public Policy	PR and Communications

Public Safety	Publishing
Railroad Manufacture	Ranching
Real Estate	Recreational Facilities & Services
Religious Institutions	Renewables and Environment
Research	Restaurants
Retail	Security and Investigations
Semiconductors	Shipbuilding
Sporting Goods	Sports
Staffing & Recruiting	Supermarkets
Telecommunications	Textiles
Think Tanks	Tobacco
Translation & Localization	Transportation/Trucking/Railroad
Utilities	Venture Capital and Private Equity
Veterinary	Warehousing
Wholesale	Wine and Spirits
Wireless	Writing and Editing

You can't connect the dots looking forward; you can only connect them looking backwards. So you have to trust that the dots will somehow connect in your future.

--Steve Jobs

Select your top five companies, those that align with your career, and, using the search bar, search for people whose profiles have those company names. Read their profiles and connect with them. Build the relationships, research their profiles, and begin to understand your Top Five companies, not from the business side, which you have already done, but from the people side. Get a feel for the people who make up the companies. Let them get to know you! They need you as much as you need them.

Yes, Barbie® has turned 57

That adorable doll that has just turned 55 and has traveled the world with more than 40 nationalities. Barbie® has had more careers than any of us can ever imagine. With over 130 careers she has been a business executive, a doctor, flown to the moon as an astronaut, worked weekends as a cashier at McDonald's, and even been an elementary school teacher. I guess you can say she can teach us a few things about careers. Barbie can also teach us a few things about social media. She plays on Facebook with 13 million fans, 240,000 Twitter followers and over 600,000 followers on Instagram.

Here are This Chapter's Business Consultant Influencers

As you read these profiles, look for possible referrals for your needs.

Is there something in their story you connect with?
Could you gain a new idea or insight for your business or career?
Who do you know or who do they know that can help both of you?
If you needed help or wanted to buy a product, what would it be?
How do you follow up when you meet someone?
When people view your profile, how do you want them to feel?
Do your tribes line up so you could be Power Partners?
What are your favorite questions to ask in an introductory call?

Brenda Cooper

Emmy Award Winning Celebrity & Executive Image Consultant / Fashion Stylist / Color Expert & Keynote Speaker

"Life isn't about finding yourself. Life is about creating yourself."
--George Bernard Shaw

Growing up in London I always had a flair for style. I came to America with just a dream, and my dream came true. With persistent effort I made an image for myself. I've had the great fortune of creating wardrobes for the Hollywood elite, winning an Emmy for my work and living my passion.

Today I am passionate about empowering men and women so that they step into their greatness. My mission is to unravel the mystery and confusion of fashion and make it available to anybody, on any budget, regardless of size, weight, height or age so that anyone can have award winning style.

►The problem is that Fashion "rules" don't work for most people. We come in too many shapes, sizes, preference and budgets. And trying to squeeze your personal style into someone else's vision of fashion can be a nightmare! I build wardrobes of attractive, modern, functional clothes that fit and flatter. It's the Aahh factor!

►So I say, instead of learning the rules, learn how to make fashion work for you! Turn fashion around. Learn how to highlight your assets (And yes, you do have assets!) Discover how to develop your own sense of style and feel what it's like to walk out the door looking terrific and feeling unstoppable every day.

►When a person finds their own personal style, wearing colors that illuminate, clothes that fit and flatter they feel on top of the world. It happens with my celebrity clients, my business executives as well as my working moms. It can happen for you too.

Specialties: Personal Color Analysis, Wardrobe Assessment & Edit, Professional Shopping, Special Event Dressing, Packing Selection for Travel, Red Carpet Dressing, Fabric and style selection for Made to Order Clothes, Inner Closet Clearing, Image Management & Development

What three books do you feel are a must that you highly recommend others to read? *The Four Agreements* by Miguel Ruiz, *How Your Child is Smart* by Dawna Markova, *Loving What IS* by Byron Katie, *NOW Discover Your Strengths* by Marcus Buckingham

What movie touched you by its meaning or inspired you? *Searching for Sugarman*, Won Best Documentary at Hollywood Oscars & British Oscars in 2012. The story of a musician who led a hard and ordinary life in Detroit unaware of his fame in South Africa where un be known to him he was more popular than Elvis or The Beatles.

What will you do differently this year from last year or what do you want more of? This year and every year for that matter going forward I want to take more actions living into my discomfort zone. I am committed to reaching my full potential in both my personal and professional life, stepping into my full unapologetic self-expression so that I can be an example for others to step into their full unapologetic self-expression! Yes!!

If you could be anyone for a day, who would it be and what experience can you envision? I would be Martin Luther King for a day to experience his commitment for a cause that was so much bigger than him for the racial equality of humanity.

What discipline could someone learn from you, that would take them to the next level, and how did you develop it? The discipline someone could learn from me to get to the next level would be the discipline of moment to moment awareness of the mind with its assumptions that hinder us from being free to be and act in any situation.

What movie makes you cry, every time you see it? It is not a movie, it's the 1997 Apple 'Think Different' Commercial Every time I watch it, I am touched moved and inspired by its profound message.

What one problem in the world would you solve? I would solve the problem of the rigid belief systems that cause in violence, cruelty, war, misdeeds and greed in the world.

Brenda's Favorite Characteristics:
Authentic, Compassionate, Curious, Compassionate, Courageous, Connected, Humorous, Imaginative, Self-Expressed

Brenda Cooper, Chief Style Officer 'Whatever you do, do it with Style!"
Emmy Award Winner, Empowering Executives & Celebrities Through the Power Of Style!
▶ style@brendacooper.com ◀ & ▶ www.brendacooper.com ◀
LinkedIn Profile: https://www.linkedin.com/in/brenda-cooper-7695a811.

Dr. Geneva J. Williams

Life Leadership Coach ~ Podcaster
Master Facilitator

"I believe your purpose in life is to better yourself and your community, and the two go hand-in-hand." Dr. Geneva J. Williams

A defining moment came when, as a teenager, my family received hate mail and had a cross on our front lawn saying, "get out" of our home in New Jersey. Inspired by my father's tireless role as courageous civil rights leader, leadership became an emphasis of my career.

Seeing my dad in action shaped my view about what you're expected to do in life: overcome the tough times, raise up, train and ignite leaders to make impact in their communities and leave a legacy of greatness.

As a master leadership strategist, I help women entrepreneurs and executives become great leaders by providing proven strategies for leading in their workplace and community. My weekly podcast, *Ignite2Impact,* is broadcast on many platforms including iHeartRadio and Apple Podcasts.

►Created youth employment and career opportunities, resulting in over $1 million, 600 jobs and national recognition as a best-practice model

► Created *Lead Your Own Life*, a series of conversations and lessons for executives and entrepreneurs who want to take their leadership to the next level.

►Generated over $100 million in government and philanthropic support for issues such as youth development and leadership, services for disadvantaged populations, workforce readiness, and economic development

SPECIALTIES: Collaboration / Leadership Development / Problem Solving/Strategic Communications / Fundraising / Fund Development / Facilitation / Podcast Host / Partnership Development / Community Organizer / Executive Coaching

Who in your childhood was a major influence that helped shape your life? My Dad. He was an ordinary man with an extraordinary ability to lead and make a difference for others.

What will you do differently this year from last year or what do you want more of? More of my photography. Dealing with the loss of my parents and husband kept me from continuing what has been a life-long hobby/passion. I learn much about life looking thru a camera lens, and capturing images thru my perspective, and then sharing with others.

Who now is a Mentor, Coach or Strategist that is on your advisory council? My housekeeper and personal trainer are my self-care advisors. Both are entrepreneurs, and listening and learning from them helps me as well.

If you could be anyone for a day, who would it be and what experience can you envision? Rosa Parks, the mother of the Civil Rights movement. I'd really want to experience how she developed her sense of purpose, coupled with her self-awareness, prior to that historic event.

What discipline could someone learn from you? How to collaborate, and work in teams and together with others. I've studied, wrote about, practiced collaboration for 30+ years.

In helping others, is it better to teach them, give them, or show them? *Helping others* is key. It's about what **others** need, how **they** learn best. Do all three: teach, give, and show.

If there were one problem in the world you could solve, what would it be? Not enough of our younger generations are prepared to step into tomorrow's leadership roles.

Geneva's Favorite Characteristics

Purpose Driven, Inspiring Leader, Tactical Problem Solver, Relationship Builder, Collaborator, Life-long learner, Facilitator

Dr. Geneva J. Williams aka *"Dr. Geneva Speaks..."*

"Inspiring Great Leaders for Greater Purpose"

♛ Life Leadership of Self, Career & in the Community ♛ Group Facilitator

♛ Podcast Radio Host ♛ Online Course Creator

✓ geneva@drgenevaspeaks.com 🔥313-312-5810 ♛

www.DrGenevaSpeaks.com ✓

The following was found written on the wall in Mother Teresa's home for children in Calcutta:

People are often unreasonable, irrational, and self-centered. Forgive them anyway.

If you are kind, people may accuse you of selfish, ulterior motives. Be kind anyway.

If you are successful, you will win some unfaithful friends and some genuine enemies. Succeed anyway.

If you are honest and sincere people may deceive you. Be honest and sincere anyway.

What you spend years creating, others could destroy overnight. Create anyway.

If you find serenity and happiness, some may be jealous. Be happy anyway.

The good you do today, will often be forgotten. Do good anyway.

Give the best you have, and it will never be enough. Give your best anyway.

In the final analysis, it is between you and God. It was never between you and them anyway.

Mother Theresa

Chapter 10
The Power of Charity and Volunteering

Let us not be satisfied with just giving money. Money is not enough, money can be got, but they need your hearts to love them. So, spread your love everywhere you go.

--Mother Teresa

▶ Jim Palmer ◀

★ Committed to Helping One Million Homeless ★ CEO
Orange County Rescue Mission a Non-Profit Organization

Orange County, California Area | Nonprofit Organization Management

Current	Hurtt Family Health Clinics a Non-Profit Organization, County of Orange Housing Authority & Community Resources, Orange County Rescue Mission
Previous	OC Partnership to End Homelessness, Corporation for National and Community Service, City of Tustin
Education	Corona del Mar High School

Send a message ▼

500+
connections

My Influencers: Jim Palmer

Have you ever tried to be neighborly but found that one of your neighbors seemed less than welcoming? You might have asked yourself, "What's wrong with them?" When this happens, we need to resist the urge to make snap assumptions. Sometimes we don't know how or why sparrows have broken wings.

One of my favorite people in the charity world is Jim Palmer. Very few people in this world understood their mission as early as Jim Palmer. At the age of 14 years old, Jim found out that his next-door neighbor could not make their house payment and were going to lose their home. The father had died, leaving the family with no

173

income. His heart bled for the children, who he thought would become homeless, and wondered where they would sleep, how they would find food, and who would protect them. That started him on his mission to help the homeless.

Karma is the eternal assertion of human freedom...Our thoughts, our words, and deeds are the threads of the net which we throw around ourselves.
--Swami Vivekananda

Charity means love. "The least, the last, and the lost." Jim Palmer's organization helps them all. Jim is the CEO of Orange County Rescue Mission, a Christian Haven helping people in Orange County get off the streets forever. When people hit bottom, they face the most difficult time of their lives. They've lost their job, their home and have nowhere to go. Orange County Rescue Mission helps them. When people show up addicted to drugs or alcohol, Orange County Rescue Mission helps them find rehab centers and takes them back after they've followed the programs. When people who had addictions and worked their way through rehab are ready to rejoin the community, Orange County Rescue Mission helps.

Each year the Mission saves over 200 lives. People know they can count on breakfast, lunch, and dinner for their children and a roof over their heads. I went to a recent graduation and listened and learned how people who had no hope, no family, even single moms with babies, were able to start over in their communities and build life skills that will help them be more productive.

The OCRM puts those who have a child to work in their daycare program. Others are given jobs inside the program with no phone privileges, specific bed times, and time windows for meals to get them back on track and put the idea of keeping a schedule back into their lives. Some of OCRM's clients graduate from two-year colleges or trade schools with skills that get them jobs as their lives go forward. These people in turn help others and create the ripple effect that saves lives.

When you make a paradigm shift to adopt the mindset that you are here to make a difference, to help the other people, your entire LinkedIn visibility will change. When you use the fundamentals, I have given you in this book, your LinkedIn profile will stand out like you paid $1,000 dollars to a professional to create it. The important part of LinkedIn is its ability to help you build relationships.

In this chapter, I will teach you to build relationships and build a profile that will make a difference to others. If you help somebody today, they will remember you in the future. It doesn't take much, but what you do will resonate with those you helped forever.

Consider adding him to your influencer list.

Attitude of Gratitude

Last year, as I was preparing to send out my annual Thanksgiving letters, I found an old letter in which I wrote about giving thanks to my friends and remembering a time when I had nothing.

One of my girlfriends went to Hawaii for three months and let me live in her condo in Santa Monica. At the time I had no job and no income. The condo was free but I was still responsible for the electricity, the gas, and the utilities.

Later, as Thanksgiving approached, I called a few of my friends to catch up. I told one of my friends that I wasn't sure what I was going to do about Thanksgiving because my oven didn't work. She told me not to worry, that she had it under control. She brought over a roasting pan (the kind that that you plug in) and a turkey and we roasted the turkey. As I reconnected with my friends in the weeks prior to Thanksgiving, everybody worked together and on the big day, all of them brought food. We created a feast fit for a king! We played games, laughed, and joked. It was the best Thanksgiving ever! It started out as a Thanksgiving where I had nothing and became an incredibly memorable day with friends and food. What more could I have asked for? I was so thankful.

When you approach life with an "attitude of gratitude" you will be surprised at how much you really do have. Changing how you look at life will drive you to be more successful than you ever imagined. Many times we look at our lives and are unhappy because we're focused on the wrong parts. Focus on the positive, have an attitude of gratitude, and be thankful for what you have.

Tony Robbins, one of my mentors, has a similar mission statement on his Tony Robbins International Basket Brigade website. It is one of the ways Tony Robbins *chooses* to make a difference: "The International Basket Brigade is built on a simple notion: one small act of generosity on the part of one caring person can transform the lives of hundreds." What began as Tony's individual effort to feed families in need has now grown to the point where his campaign provides baskets of food and household items for an estimated two million people annually in countries all over the world.

Compassion will cure more sins than condemnation.
--Henry Ward Beecher

I'm reminded of my friend, motivational speaker and author Michael J. Herman, who shared a story with me about one Christmas Eve when he and his wife Penny filled up their car with food and from the back of their car fed 68 homeless and hungry people living on Skid Row. Out of that experience of altruism and while creating a project to benefit the community through Landmark Education's Self Expression and Leadership Course, Herman's program, The Needy Smorgasbord Project, was born.

The next Christmas Eve, Herman and his wife brought an army of more than 100 friends and volunteers along with donations from almost 50 restaurants and stores to feed homeless, hungry, and needy people. Now this nationwide movement reaches tens of thousands in need. The outcomes were possible because Herman sought to help others. This story of generosity touched me so much that I invited Michael to partner with me on a book about giving and philanthropy.

Can you see how little movements like these can change the world? Can you see how you have within you the greatness and the power to build structures and systems for change and abundance?

Yes, you do!

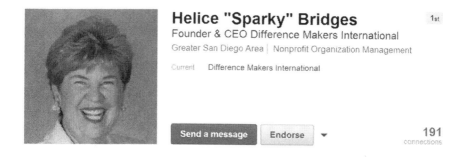

Helice "Sparky" Bridges
1st

Founder & CEO Difference Makers International
Greater San Diego Area | Nonprofit Organization Management

Current   Difference Makers International

Send a message   Endorse   ▼

191
connections

You Have a Calling

Like random acts of kindness, being at the right place at the right time is critical. My mentor coach Bob Donnell invited me to his inner circle where I met a personality as big as her nickname, Sparky. She gave me a huge heart hug.

"In 1979," she told me, "I was married, had two pre-teen sons, a successful career and a beautiful home overlooking the Pacific Ocean. But no matter how much money I made, I had to live with a husband who controlled, intimidated and verbally abusive me. I was spiritually and emotionally broken. I had no way out. On the very day I decided to commit suicide, I heard a voice inside me say, "You cannot take your life because you are going to make a big difference in the world."

That changed her life. After she divorced her husband, she founded Difference Makers International and created a way to show people how to express appreciation, respect and love for themselves and others which has impacted over 40 million people throughout the world, eradicating bullying, preventing adolescent suicide and helping make dreams come true. She has just launched a global project – One Billion Dreams Coming True by 2020.

Random Acts of Kindness

Since one of my mentors has always been Mother Teresa, I have a huge compassion for the homeless.

I don't if anybody knows the actual percentage of homeless people who are mentally ill. Still, it breaks my heart that they don't know how to properly take care of or fend for themselves. When we care for each other, it's hard for us to see someone else suffering and in need and not take some kind of action.

Since you get more joy out of giving joy to others, you should put a good deal of thought into the happiness that you are able to give.
--Eleanor Roosevelt

One time I was driving by McDonald's and realized my dog needed water so I ran in quickly to get him some water. Before I could open the door to the restaurant, I saw a homeless woman with different color socks, wearing a poncho, unkempt hair, with a shopping cart filled with her treasures, items others would see as junk.

I instantly stopped and asked her if she was hungry. We caught each other's eyes and she said yes. I thought that buying this woman a meal would be an easy task for me. However, I realized I hadn't gone to the bank and I was standing there with no cash and no debit card.

I decided to use my resourcefulness and ask the cashier if she might have something she could give to this homeless person. She said no. I explained to the cashier that I had no money on me but this woman was hungry and homeless. She said no again. I asked to see the manager.

The manager came out from behind the counter and in an abrupt manner said, "What do you want?"

I said to him, "There's a homeless woman here who's hungry. You must have something here that can help her. You must have something in the warmer that isn't on order."

He again said no.

"Do you understand that this is a human being who lives in your community? I find it hard to believe you would let someone go hungry."

 Volunteer Experience & Causes

Co-Chair
Afghan Amity Society fundraiser
January 2010 – August 2012 (2 years 8 months) | Children

Co-Chair Laguna Beach for Afghan Amity Society fundraiser. Arranged for 20 artists for event with speaker, world renowned humanist Dr. Masaru Emaoto. Afghan Amity has now helped over 600 women and children in Herat, Afghanistan, to get an education and clean, healthy water to villages in Afghanistan. Can you imagine... If we could get clean water to all that need, we would save 2 million lives a year.

Opportunities you are looking for:

• Joining a nonprofit board

Causes you care about:

• Animal Welfare
• Children
• Economic Empowerment
• Education
• Human Rights
• Women protection against Domestic Violence
• Protecting Wild Life
• Arts & Music for Children
• Homeless with Mental Illness
• Creating Leaders for the Next Generation

Organizations you support:

• Orange County Rescue Mission
• Best Friends Animal Society
• Disabled American Veterans
• Helping Children Worldwide
• Special Olympics
• NAMI
• A Mission For Michael

He said, "It's our policy."

At this point I found myself so frustrated with McDonald's that I started to ask the patrons in the store if they wanted to contribute to buy her lunch. While the woman stood next to me with a sad expression on her face, I asked four tables for help and could not get one person to say yes. I looked at a man who had three cheeseburgers on his tray and asked if he wanted to give her one. He said no.

I have found that among its other benefits, giving liberates the soul of the giver.
--Maya Angelou

At this point I was beginning to feel like a failure. All I wanted to do was feed someone who had no food and I couldn't even help this one poor woman. My frantic energy must have been bouncing off the walls. In the distance, I saw an Asian couple and heard them speaking to each other but I couldn't understand them. For whatever reason, I hadn't bothered to ask them for help knowing it might be difficult for them to understand me.

However, they did understand my desperate desire. The woman stood and walked over to me and said, "...food...she food...she food?" She pointed at the food and then at the homeless lady.

I said, "Yes, yes," nodding my head up and down.

She said, "I I I," and tapped her chest. All I could say was thank you.

As I watched, the lady told the man, "Meal meal meal," then walked to the counter and bought the homeless lady a meal.

The lady looked at the Asian woman and said, "God bless you."

What's your cause? Helping the homeless, working with underprivileged children, and working with animals that have been rescued are just a few of the causes supported by thousands of charity organizations you can get involved with. Decide what pulls at your heart strings the most and then commit to helping others.

One of my favorite things to do is always carry a protein bar in my glove box. It's simple and easy and it doesn't matter where I am. If I pull into a shopping center and see a homeless person sitting there, I say, "Hey, I have one of these great protein bars. Do you want one?" They almost always say yes.

One day I was eating at a pancake house with my daughter and our breakfast cost $15, which left me with $10. We figured our meal was cheap but her service was extremely top-notch so we left her the

$10 and said, "Thanks! You made our morning delightful." She smiled and said, "You made mine off to a great start."

When we walked out the door we saw a homeless man lying on the grass. He had no socks and his shoes were so worn they looked like they were going to fall off his feet. His hair and beard were both matted and dirty, but through his tattered and torn clothes you could tell they were hanging loose on his body, an indication of malnutrition. It broke my heart, but I had given the waitress the last of my money. I looked around to see if there was another way I could get help for him.

Winners never quit and quitters never win.
--Vince Lombardi

Five different sets of people were standing outside the restaurant waiting for their name to get called to eat their breakfast. I went from family to family asking, "Do you see that homeless man over there? Would you be willing to give him a couple bucks so he could get something to eat?" One by one they all either said no or turned away, I got so frustrated that people who were going to fill their bellies would allow someone to go hungry right in front of them.

Finally, the door opened and out walked a very young couple. They looked like they were in love or certainly were having a very nice time. I felt silly asking them because it was probably a treat for them to spend the money to go out to breakfast.

I asked anyway. The young man said, "We just used our debit card."

I got it, but then I noticed that they had taken their leftovers. I said, "I know this sounds weird, but do you really think you'll eat those leftovers? I know half the time I think I will eat them but half the time I don't. Why don't you go over there and ask him if he wants them?"

Thoughts and Tips

Pay the toll for the person behind you.

When someone is digging for change, pay it for them.

Pay for someone's car wash.

I had done what I could and walked back to my car. As I got to my car I looked back and saw the homeless guy already eating the food. I smiled ear to ear. I turned the car on, pulled out of the parking lot, and drove down the street. Just as I was about to make a U-turn I heard a honk-honk-honk. It was the young couple, my giving sweet new human connections, waving to me. I could feel their smile and their happiness that they knew they had made a difference.

Later my daughter said, "You know how to bring the best out in people."

I said, "They had greatness in them. "

Even corporations are doing these random acts.

Honda shifted to a Charity message of Random Acts of Helpfulness in its advertising. This brought Honda to the forefront by increasing consumer trust. Local dealer employees went out to the community and washed people's cars, brought nurse, donated needed baby items, and paid for people's parking, while wearing branded light blue polo shirts. They left behind little notes saying, "It's on us." Your Helpful Honda Dealers.

With greater fuel economy and more reliability, small autos have become more popular. JD Power and AARP discovered that people in the 50+ demographic fuel over 60% of US car sales. Honda's new charity message reaches the people who are most likely to buy their cars.

Pay it forward. "Making a Difference"

What has someone done for you in the past that you can do for someone else today? Years ago, I planned to take a trip from California to Chicago, Illinois. I would fly to Chicago and take the train from the airport to my destination.

You can give without loving, but you can never love without giving.
--Robert Louis Stevenson

At that time, I was young and had lived in California most of my life. I was single and was much more concerned to look cute than with the weather. I never even thought about the fact that it was the middle of winter. What did I know about snow? So I arrived in Chicago wearing a darling black leather jacket and matching skirt and shoes and transferred from the airport to the train, all without stepping outside. When I arrived at the train station in downtown Chicago I was suddenly outside in 30-degree weather shivering like a chattering monkey.

A lady twice my age said, "Oh my dear, you must be cold."

I was grateful she didn't say, "What in the world are you doing wearing that?" I tried a bit of a laugh and slowly said, "Yeah."

She asked, "Where are you from?"

I said, "Ca-ca-calif-for-ni-a."

She said, "No wonder you are cold." She reached into her bag and said, "Then you must take these."

She pulled out a pair of suede black gloves and handed them to me. To this day I feel like she must have been a guardian angel looking out for me.

Now I know that when the weather gets cold, go to the 99 Cent store where they have two pairs of gloves for $1, grab a bunch and give them to people who look like they need them. Believe me, the smiles they give me are way more valuable than the dollar I spent to help them.

Together we are more

Dee Beaudette
President at Collective Changes, dedicated to supporting global women entrepreneurs through education and mentoring
Greater Seattle Area | Nonprofit Organization Management

Current	Collective Changes, Dee Beaudette Consulting, MacKenzie Romero Consulting
Previous	Peak Education, HIS Foundation, Webster International
Education	Independent Study - AFP Faculty Certification

Send a message   Endorse ▾   500+ connections

Gail M. Romero, CFRE
CEO Collective Changes, NACC Past Board Chair, BM Gates Foundation - Advisor, Senior Counsel MacKenzie-Romero Consult
Greater Seattle Area | Executive Office

Current	Bill & Melinda Gates Foundation, Collective Changes - Global Mentoring, Rainmakers tv
Previous	MBA Women International, MBA Women International - formerly NAWMBA, Growing Philanthropy Summit
Education	AFP Faculty Training Academy

Connect   Send Gail InMail ▾   500+ connections

Anytime I go somewhere I keep my ears open and my antennae up. I got an opportunity to go a very large women's conference in Long Beach, produced by Michelle Paterson and formerly produced by Maria Shriver in Long Beach.

> *If you're trying to achieve, there will be roadblocks. I've had them;*
> *everybody has had them. But obstacles don't have to stop you. If you run*
> *into a wall, don't around and give up. Figure out how to climb it, go*
> *through it, or work around it.*
> **--Michael Jordan**

Among the amazing speakers were Jack Canfield and Lisa Nichols. At one of the booths, I saw a banner that said Collective Changes and curiosity struck. "What was this odd thing about?" I thought. I saw the opportunity, reached out my hand, and said, "Hi, my name is Debra Faris, what's yours?" That's how I met Dee Beaudette.

I was excited as she told me about how Collective Changes became a Global non-profit corporation that empowers women in business through collaboration. "We use a unique on-line and mobile technology to match mentors and mentees. Then we guide them through tasks that build leadership and business skills," she said. "We launched in South Africa and then expanded to help women around the world build and sustain enterprises that create social, political and economic stability."

Dee met Gail in an on-line Master's program at Northpark University in Chicago. Since they both lived on the West Coast, they teamed up to do group projects. After eight years working in different cities, they decided to reconnect and follow their passion for empowering women. Collective Changes was born.

Collective Changes' primary target audience is the forgotten middle women in emerging countries who owning small to medium size enterprises. They complete a six-month program, then continue as associate and then full mentors building leadership skills in their communities.

Social media is an amazing tool, but it's really the face-to-face interaction that makes a long-term impact.

--Felicia Day

Here are This Chapter's Business Consultant Influencers

As you read these profiles, look for possible referrals for your needs.

Is there something in their story you connect with?

Could you gain a new idea or insight for your business or career?

Who do you know or who do they know that can help both of you?

If you needed help or wanted to buy a product, what would it be?

How do you follow up when you meet someone?

When people view your profile, how do you want them to feel?

Do your tribes line up so you could be Power Partners?

What are your favorite questions to ask in an introductory call?

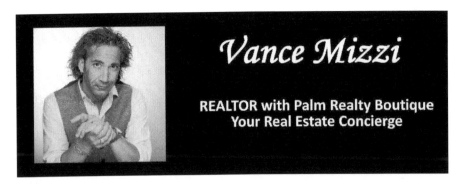

"I not only sell the lifestyle... I'm living the dream." ~ Vance Mizzi

As a kid growing up on Long Island I dreamt of living in Los Angeles. In the early 90's as a young 20 something I followed my dream and moved west. For years I worked in a service based industry that put me in front of celebrities along with the elite of Hollywood and Beverly Hills. Throughout the 90's there wasn't a famous or influential person that I didn't get to know in the areas of entertainment and music. I learned how to identify with them as people and how to work with them in a confidential one-to-one basis. Later I moved back to New York and spent 10 years on Wall Street as a Financial Planner. There I learned to understand the importance of other people's money, how they viewed their investments and sharpened my skills as a negotiator.

In 2009 I formed the Mizzi Group. A corporation dedicated to providing top level representation for clients whether buying or selling luxury real estate. Utilizing my team's expertise, and my personal communication skills we've managed to break records in the Los Angeles Real Estate Market all while keeping our clients' best interests in the forefront.

Our Mission Statement is to

▶ Provide an unprecedented Concierge experience for our clients

▶ Pledge to be in constant communication with our clients, keeping them fully informed throughout the entire buying or selling process

▶ Measure success through the satisfaction of our clients

Specialties: Luxury Homes / Beachfront Properties / Luxury Leasing / Investors / 1031 Exchange / Real Estate Development / Distressed Properties / International Referrals / Executive Relocation

What three books do you feel are a must that you highly recommend others to read? Three books: *Think and Grow Rich, The Big Leap and High-Performance Habits*.

What movie touched you by its meaning or inspired you? Movie: *Rocky* You need to believe in yourself and desire to go the distance.

What will you do differently this year from last year or what do you want more of? Different or more of: Last year I spent an enormous amount of time on self-development, it helped shape my attitude and actions. This year I plan to spend equal or more time attending seminars and workshops developing myself to be at top physical and mental form.

Who now is a Mentor, Coach or Strategist that is on your advisory council? Mentor, Strategist, Coach: My wife Maria, we have been together for over 27 years and have experienced every high and low one could imagine. We support one another in everything we do and continue to learn from one each other.

What discipline could someone learn from you? Discipline: My ability to do what I put my mind to. Once a decision is made to act on something, I am very focused and determined to get the result I set out for.

When "winning someone over" do you think facts or emotions carry the day? Winning someone over: When arguing or discussing a topic one always needs to keep in mind that facts tell but stories sell. You need to empathize and identify with your counterpart in order to win them over. By changing the way you look at things the things you look change.

In helping others, is it better to teach them, give them, or show them? Helping others: It is a gift to be of assistance to someone or some type of cause. That ability to make a difference or be the difference in someone's life is personally life altering. To teach someone self-reliance is the biggest gift you can give to anyone.

Vance's Favorite Characteristics

Fiscally Responsible, Strong Communicator, Good Listener, Shrewd Negotiator, Focused, Team Leader, Motivator, Strong Minded, Confidential, Honest, High-Level Industry Knowledge & Property Values, Approachable, Generous

Vance Mizzi **aka** "The Luxury Real Estate Concierge""We Move People"
♛ Luxury Residential Real Estate ♕ Beachfront Real Estate ♛ One-to-One-Real Estate Concierge ♕ Real Estate Negotiating Specialist
♜ Vance@TheMizziGroup.com ♟ 424-634-8492 ♛ TheMizziGroup.com✓

Suzette Febre Hart

Mentor, Educator, Mom

"It is, what it is." Unknown Author

My life changed dramatically when my 23-year-old older sister & best friend died unexpectedly in a car crash. Before then, I graduated early from high school and achieved the 2-year Fashion Institute of Technology Certification. I immediately landed a position at the Super Gap and opened numerous stores from the ground floor up.

After my sister's death I was unable to do anything but lay around for 6 months, and my family was concerned for me. They and a family friend, Henning Morales, strongly encouraged me to go back to school. I did so and was mentored by my English Professor, Dr Leo Thorne. Both Leo and Henning helped me put my life back together, and we continue to be friends and work on projects together. This experience taught me the power of receiving a second chance.

Today, I'm a retired English & ELS teacher that included teaching K-12 at various schools including East Side which was the setting of a movie.

I created MEM to give back, and I co-founded the Youth Mentorship Forum in January 2017. Our mission is to address the issues and challenges facing today's youth through Education, Mentoring and Coaching. We're currently working on getting this program into the school system and funding for the project.

▶ Professionals
▶ Young Adults, Parents, Educators
▶ Those Struggling in Life

SPECIALTIES: Educator, Writer, Author, Mentor

Suzette's Favorite Characteristics
Tenacious, Compassionate, Knowledgeable, Motivated, Intuitive,
Enthusiastic

Dr. Suzette Febre aka *"Mentor, Educator, Mom"* MEM (with Heart)
"Educating, Mentoring & Coaching Today's Youth"
♛ Non-Profit Mentorship ♛ Author ♟ Speaker Forums
♜ suzette@drsuzettefebre.com ♟ 201-390-0978 ♛
www.drsuzettefebre.com ✓

Troy Hoffman

Founder / CEO Simpluris, Inc.
"We help You"
Class Action Settlement Administration

"Questions provide the key to unlocking our unlimited potential." ~
Anthony Robbins

I have always had a drive to "Make a Difference & Help Others" combined with a work ethic of quitting time is when the job is done. The Entrepreneur bug got into me when I was 12 years old. I started "Suds Brothers" Car Detailing Service, passed out homemade flyers, and the business started rolling in. Since then, I built multiple companies. Along the way, I have been extremely blessed to have incredible Mentors in my life that have poured all of their knowledge and wisdom into me. I was able to found an amazing company with great leaders, which gave me the ability to build an incredible organization from the ground up to a national scale.

I Founded, Simpluris, Inc. in 2007. It has rapidly grown to 70+ employees, with offices in 3 states; (CA TX & FL) and has administered over 2,000 Settlements and Noticing procedures. This outstanding growth and success was recently recognized by Inc. Magazine; which ranked Simpluris, Inc. at #171 on its 30th annual Inc. 500 list; an exclusive ranking of the nation's fastest growing private companies in 2011, 2012, & 2013

AREAS OF PRACTICE: ▶ ADA / American's Disabilities Act / Antitrust / Banking / Civil Rights / Consumer / Coupon / Discrimination / Employment / Environmental / Finance / Healthcare / Insurance / Mass Tort / Personal Injury / Product / Product Liability / Securities / Specialty Areas / Wage and Hour

SERVICES & SOLUTIONS: ▶ Bankruptcy Case Administration / Call Center / Case Websites / Claims Processing / Class Action Settlement Administration / Class Member Tracking / Data Management / Fund Distribution and Tax Reporting / Litigation Support / Notice of Class Certification / Reporting Statistics / Secure Mailing Campaigns.

What three books do you feel are a must that you highly recommend others to read? *Warrior Book, Mastering the Rockefeller Habits, Crucial Conversations*

What movie touched you by its meaning or inspired you? *Braveheart... Live LIFE WITH PASSION!*

Who in your childhood was a major influence that helped shape your life? I was blessed to have a father who was a true Mans Man... He built his own Electrical Contracting company. Then became a Chiropractor, Internal Medicinist, Clinical Nutritionist, and Neurologist. Watching him learn and then apply in massive ways was huge for me. Any obstacle can be figured out if you put your mind to it.

What discipline could someone learn from you? I deeply connect with true heart with people and truly care. I try not to judge and help everyone I can. It's not for personal gain. Just the way I was raised to care for and help those around you.

When "winning someone over" do you think facts or emotions carry the day? Winning people over is more about just listening and connecting. Most people don't care who you are or what you have done. They just want real connection with someone that will listen, and they feel really cares.

What do you wish you spent more time doing? What prevents you from doing that now? I wish I spent more time implementing all that I've learned. With so many things Ive learned just applying daily requires 6-9 hours a day... and with building a company. It's definitely not easy applying it all. To truly help you need to shift their stories they are telling themselves and open them up to new possibilities. From there anything is possible if they BELIEVE.

Troy's Favorite Characteristics
Making a Difference, Leadership, Serving Others, Trustworthy, Innovative

Troy Hoffman ~ "Always Client Focused"
"Meticulous Class Action Settlement Administrators"
Helping Attorney's & Law Firms WorldWide
▶thoffman@Simpluris.com ◀ ▶800-779-2104◀

Chapter 11
Success Leaves a Trail

It someone offers you an amazing opportunity and you are not sure you can do it, say yes – then learn how to do it later.
--Richard Branson

Richard Branson
Founder at Virgin Group
Virgin Islands (British)   Aviation & Aerospace
Education   Stowe School

in fluencer

9,195,061
followers

My Influencers: Richard Branson

Recently, I was having a friendly conversation with my good friend Lee Pound and we were talking about Richard Branson and loving his quote about saying yes to opportunity and then learning how do the job. Lee chuckled and said, "Very early in my career, I was asked to be a newspaper editor. I had never been one except for three months in college. Another time I was asked to be a controller with no accounting background whatsoever. I took the job and figured it out and did it for three years until they sold the company. Two months later, the new owner's CFO quit and I became CFO of a public corporation. I never took an accounting course and was not a CPA but I did it anyway and kept that job for over 20 years."

Yeah Yeah Yeah... Who Doesn't love Richard Branson, multi-billionaire, with a wife he has adored for 40 years, who lives on an island he bought for 180k that's now worth 200 million (not a bad investment)? But he didn't always have everything. Even his wife prior to marrying him was probably wondering what she was getting herself into. There's something about an entrepreneur that's different. Some claim it's in their DNA. Even I was called a bird of a different color; most entrepreneurs are. Entrepreneurs aren't always attached to money… but driven, yes, wildly imaginative, and out of the box thinkers… yes, yes, yes! That's probably why I love his sense of human kindness, wanting to create extraordinary things and change the world.

Coming together is a beginning; keeping together is a progress; Working together is success.
--Henry Ford

Shortly after high school, I found this coupon where I could get three magazines for the price of one. I remember two of them, one was *Entrepreneur* magazine and the other was *Black Enterprise*. They both featured summaries of most of the great development and self-help books so you didn't have to read a whole book. They featured amazing successful entrepreneurs like Richard Branson in bite-size pieces. As Brian Tracy noted, "How do you eat an elephant? One bite at a time."

I am telling you to make a choice based on your passions and interests, not what everyone else is telling you to do. It doesn't work that way. You wind up living a life for the wrong reasons, and you never get the most out of it. Just always think about why you are doing what you are doing.
--Jeff Hoffman

Later, I found out Richard Branson actually started his entrepreneurship with a magazine called *Student* at the age of 16. I often wondered if that subconsciously my own first publishing venture, *LinkedIn for College Students*.

Branson is a genuine, extraordinary man who has created, retooled, innovated, negotiated, co-created his life experiences to the highest level, as an influencer and mentor. He is an investor and philanthropist who best known as the founder of Virgin Group, which includes more than 400 companies and is worth over $5 billion. He helped thousands of people, notably Sara Blakely, the founder of Spanx, which made her the youngest female billionaire.

Each day Richard Branson influences 9,000,000 followers on LinkedIn. Are you one of them?

Looking Outside the Box

Thinking outside the box is a key to success. When you are creative as you work on your career, you will find solutions and answers others won't bother to seek out for themselves.

Earlier in this book I showed you that questions are the answer. If you understand this aphorism, it will change your world. It's not what you know that's important; it's what you don't know that you need to know that will be critical to your success. Ask yourself questions about where you want to work and what type of work you want to do. Then dig for solutions. Use LinkedIn to help in your quest. You will have millions of people, industries, jobs, and employers at your fingertips. Use your ingenuity and the relationships that you've built find new solutions to old problems. If I reach out to the CEO, will he answer me? These are a few examples of questions you can ask yourself to begin thinking outside the box and setting up your life in the manner you desire.

When you search for your next job, LinkedIn gives you a detailed roadmap that will guide you through the maze of companies where you could play your desired role.

Questions are the Answer

When I go to an event, I always ask myself what the most important thing I learned was. At a Tony Robbins seminar 20 years ago, I learned a set of questions and a mindset that I still use today: What is your purpose, what is your intention, and questions are the answers.

Here's how you do it differently. You ask yourself, "What's my purpose and what's my intention?" Your answer might be, "My purpose is to meet people I can build relationships with that further my purpose to find a job for a client."

Discipline is the bridge between goals and accomplishment.
--Jim Rohn

Is that part of your intention? No. Your intention might be, "I'm going to look for ways in which I can better serve my clients so I've compiled a list of 20 things I did in the past that didn't help my clients."

When you do this, ask, "What are the questions that I can ask a person attending this event?" That would be far more productive. One of Stephen Covey's most important mindsets is, "First seek to understand then to be understood." If you invest in the people you want to meet and help and not in your own story, you will be far more successful.

Recently, I transformed a client's job-seeking world from networking for two years with no success to getting a job within 60 days. Here is how I did it. I asked an audience, "How many of you go to networking events?" I knew the answer. They all raised their hands and said they network. The error they make is that networking is not the end; it's a means to the end. It gives you the opportunity to meet people and build relationships. True networking results from qualifying and building the relationships you start at the networking event.

Questions are the answer to your problems. They are everything. No matter where you go, it is all about the questions. If your intention is find members of your market, start asking questions that will draw the people you are trying to attract to you.

When Tony Robbins taught me about questions and answers, he instilled in me the idea that we have to ask the right questions of ourselves and of others to get the best possible answers. When you do this right, you will forge the strongest possible relationships with others and with yourself.

The best investment you can make in yourself is getting to know yourself. Read books, take risks, and get involved in clubs that will teach you leadership. There you will discover the skills you do and do not possess and which skills you must acquire.

Jack Canfield says, "Everything you want in life is just outside your comfort zone." Step outside your normal circle of friends, your normal habits, and your normal cycle. Stretch yourself and then ask yourself how the experience felt. Analyze it by asking yourself if it made you feel inferior in some areas and superior in others. By doing this you learn and grow. You can then bring these lessons to the table when you go on interviews or sales calls.

What is ROI vs. ROT

In the finance and investment world, everyone thinks return on your investment (ROI). In the networking world, people will network and network and have nothing to show for the time invested. They neglect that most important metric, Return on Your Time (ROT).

Here is the full story of how I transformed a friend's job seeking world from networking for two years with no results to getting a job within 60 days.

Since I know a lot of people who don't take their networking to a deep enough level or qualify the time spent against the results achieved, I quickly recognized his problem.

I asked my friend, "How many networking events do you go to a week?"

He answered, "Five to seven."

I asked him, "What does your wife say when you get home?"

He answered, "She asks me how it went."

I asked, "And your reply?"

"Okay."

"*Wow!*" I said. "Let's do the math. Say you attend three events a week and it takes you an hour and half to get ready and to drive there. Is that fair?"

He said, "Yes."

I said, "You probably spend at least an hour and a half, right? That's about 12 hours a week looking for a job, and you only worked with three events."

This shows that with an effective profile on LinkedIn and connections in place, you can reach hundreds of companies in a short period of time. With recommendations from former colleagues and bosses, influencers who share your vision, and endorsements for your skills, potential employers will get a feel for who you are, to what you're committed and whether you're a good fit for their organization or not. In the current job market, as in every past era, the best way to get a job is to find a connection with more celebrity in your field than you have who can promote you inside a company or who has connections inside the company.

Internet searches and posting resumes to hundreds of companies is a thing of the past. Using your connections and resources is the way to get your next job. Through the networking and profiling available on LinkedIn, you will be ahead of the others.

Strategize your Success

When McDonald's spends a million dollars to build a new store, they position it carefully, on a corner if possible, near an intersection if they can, so it is easily visible to oncoming traffic. If you sit at a traffic light for one or two minutes, your brain may notice a McDonald's down the road and say, "McDonald's! I'm hungry!"

Many times people find themselves in the parking lot of a McDonald's or other fast food place they had no intention of visiting. Very few of them leave the house saying, "I'm going to McDonald's today," but they wind up there anyway.

Some people know that if they plan to eat a healthy lunch, they need to pack their lunch; which means planning ahead and buying healthy foods. When people make this commitment, they know what their bodies need and make health a high-level value.

Both of these examples represent a strategic plan. McDonald's uses strategy to place its restaurants in the right spot to get people to stop. The person who packs their lunch uses a different strategy. To succeed in life, you too must adopt a strategy.

The same thing happens on LinkedIn. To be successful using LinkedIn you must adopt a strategy. Yours may differ from your roommate's. Start with the end in mind, work backwards and let LinkedIn work for you. Use the strategies I have outlined in this book to build a plan to connect with the best people in your industry, develop local and the national celebrity connections, use those connections to get in the door, then let your knowledge and ideas sine in the interview that will land you your ideal job.

Who's Your Wingman?

One of my favorite movies from the 80's, *Top Gun,* depicts this next concept very nicely. The movie pairs Maverick, an egotistical fighter pilot, with Goose, his co-pilot/navigator. The two are inseparable. They compete with another pair of aviators at the top of their game as well, led by Iceman. Maverick and Iceman are rivals who don't care for each other. They have extremely different styles, different agendas, and clash at every opportunity. By the end of the movie, the two have resolved their differences and come to acknowledge that each has valuable skills. One of the best lines comes from Maverick after they've engaged in a dogfight with enemy aircraft. He looks at Ice and says, "You can be my wingman any time." Ice responds with, "No, you can be mine!" It shows that the two have figured out how to work together and to succeed.

Your wingman is a person you can count on, who is willing to take great risks for you, and who will ensure that you reach your ultimate goal. Who is your wingman? Like Maverick and Ice, you may start out rocky, but develop a bond that is strong and able to withstand anything. Develop strong, lasting relationships through LinkedIn and you will find that your wingmen will help you get the job you seek.

Social Trailblazers

Social media is social business. There's a misconception that LinkedIn isn't social media and can be used only as a business network. However, like Facebook, LinkedIn is used to connect with others and start conversations and is an acceptable form of social media.

Good leadership consists of showing average people how to do the work of superior people.
--John D. Rockefeller

People have been in the business of being social since business began. From playing golf with doctors to weekend cocktail parties at the office, the social aspect is a huge part of business. With the addition of the Internet, social interactions have stepped onto a whole new platform and expanded to include multi-media sites that make it easier than ever to reach people globally. Each platform has its strengths in different industries and genres. Some of my friends on different platforms are highly successful business people.

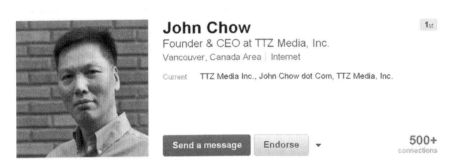

John Chow   1st
Founder & CEO at TTZ Media, Inc.
Vancouver, Canada Area | Internet

Current   TTZ Media Inc., John Chow dot Com, TTZ Media, Inc.

Send a message   Endorse   ▼   500+
                                          connections

We all know how popular blogging has become. From Fortune 500 companies to our favorite health television show, Dr. Oz, everyone is blogging or reading blogs, most of them on WordPress.

My favorite blogger is my friend John Chow, who I have lunch with on a regular basis and whose daughter plays with my dog from time to time. John talks about everyday stuff on his blog. Several times, I've seen him post photos of his lunch on his blog.

Smart phones and social media expand our universe. We can connect with others or collect information easier and faster than ever.

--Daniel Goleman

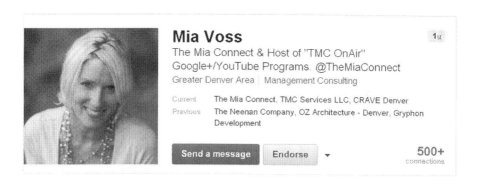

My favorite Facebook person is Mari Smith, who wrote *Facebook for Dummies.*

As we move further into the twenty-first century, the internet will continue to become more and more a way to communicate, network, and build relationships. Although each site is designed with a specific purpose, in general they all work to connect people and share communications with others.

Joel Comm

New York Times Best-Selling Author | International Keynote Speaker | Entrepreneur | New Media Marketing Strategist

Greater Denver Area | Information Technology and Services

Current	Joel Comm, Inc., a Joel Comm Company	International Conference & Keynote Speaker	Corporate Events, InfoMediaInc.com, a Joel Comm Company; Joel Comm is an International Public Keynote Speaker
Previous	Digital Future, Inc., a Joel Comm Company; Joel is an international motivational speaker, ClassicGames.com	Acquired by Yahoo as Yahoo! Games (Joel is now a keynote & motivational speaker)
Education	University of Illinois at Urbana-Champaign

Send a message ▼   500+

In the Twitter world, blogging is content driven with short and sweet tweets, tiny snippets ending with a hash tag or a link. Twitter is very popular in the job world. Joel Com uses Twitter very effectively for his business. In the Google Plus world they love their Google hangouts and You Tube.

Jack C Crawford

Senior Director at Cognizant Technology Solutions ∴.
Advisory Consultant, Customer Solutions Practice

Greater Los Angeles Area | Information Technology and Services

Current	Cognizant Technology Solutions
Previous	Allergan, 2-1-1 Orange County, OC Partnership to End Homelessness
Education	Claremont Graduate University

Send a message ▼   500+
connections

My dear friend Jack Crawford uses Google Plus regularly and speaks to and interviews many people through Google Hangouts. Mia Voss uses Google Hangouts for interviews and meetings. You can use your media link from You Tube to post interviews for Google Hangout on your LinkedIn profile.

Here are This Chapter's Business Consultant Influencers

As you read these profiles, look for possible referrals for your needs.

Is there something in their story you connect with?
Could you gain a new idea or insight for your business or career?
Who do you know or who do they know that can help both of you?
If you needed help or wanted to buy a product, what would it be?
How do you follow up when you meet someone?
When people view your profile, how do you want them to feel?
Do your tribes line up so you could be Power Partners?
What are your favorite questions to ask in an introductory call?

"Christina, you are the female Ray Kroc. (McDonalds Founder)"
~ Mark Huckins, co-founder Mr. Miniblind

I was a skinny, tall 10-year old with the will of a lion. One evening I was watching *Popeye and His Pals*, while my parents were having a party. Mom came into the den to watch the show, "I want to compete against him, the limbo champion." She replied, "Sure, whatever you say", in disbelief. Dad built a limbo pole and I practiced daily after school. Last hurdle, I had to win a limbo contest to be invited on the show. I organized a contest at school, won it and two months later I was on national TV for 5 weeks! I became the World Limbo Champion, going under 5 ½" (Coke bottle is 7 7/8") against the adult world champion from Nassau.

This experience shaped my "Can Have & Do Anything in Life Attitude". Visualization, focus and my will to win made it happen. People ask me where does this motivation and drive come from? It's part of my belief system, "I Believe" it's that simple. Persist, Persevere and You Will Prevail.

I brought my two mentors together, Anthony Robbins and Fred DeLuca, Subway Sandwich Founder. These men taught me unique knowledge that you cannot learn in textbooks. My years of involvement with Robbins was like a treasure hunt, I discovered myself deeper, learned to love public speaking and now share his golden nuggets to others. Thank you, Tony!

▶ Executives, Elevate Your Business Through Franchising
▶ Franchise, Licensing or Company Owned Operations

Specialties: Strategic Planning, Infrastructure Correction, Leadership Building, Franchise Development, Domestic & International

"I will not let anyone walk through my mind with their dirty feet"
~ Mahatma Gandhi

What three books do you feel are a must that you highly recommend others to read? *Kane & Abel*, Jeffrey Archer, *Made to Stick*, Chip & Dan Heath, *Offerings*, Danielle & Olivier Follmi

What movie touched you by its meaning or inspired you? *Remember the Titans*, Denzel Washington, team building movie

Who in your childhood was a major influence that helped shape your life? My Mother inspired me and was my best friend too.

What discipline could someone learn from you? Discipline to be grateful and trust in a higher power when the chips are down.

What do you wish you spent more time doing? What prevents you from doing that now? Playing tournament poker, it's not my time yet.

If you could be anyone for a day, who would it be and what experience can you envision? For one day, I would like to be a black jaguar, experience jungle life through their eyes.

What movie makes you cry, every time you see it? The movie *The Life of Pi*, powerful messages.

Christina's Favorite Characteristics
Analytic, Strategic, Visionary, Empowering, Entrepreneurship

Christina Kotula, aka Franchisee Expert
"Duplicate Your Blueprint, Let's Get Ready to Franchise!"
♕ Franchising Professional, Analysis of your Business
♕ Infrastructure Correction, Business Development, National Speaker ♕
♜ christina.kotula@gmail.com ♟ 949.289.3196 ♛

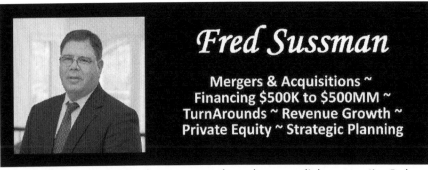

Fred Sussman

Mergers & Acquisitions ~
Financing $500K to $500MM ~
TurnArounds ~ Revenue Growth ~
Private Equity ~ Strategic Planning

Discipline is the bridge between goals and accomplishments. Jim Rohn

My father's family came from Germany in the 1930's to the Midwest. We struggled financially, my father working long hours and my mother working 3 jobs. Due to this, I became resourceful and a problem solver. I learned to listen carefully, question thoughtfully and see solutions between the lines.

Today, I am an M&A advisor and Business consultant with expertise in non-bank financing, restructuring and business growth. I have personally built and sold five businesses, two of them to public companies. My desire is to bring focus to your organization by applying proven success models, ask you the tough questions and hold you accountable for your success.

▶M & A: Acquisition and integration of 14 acquired businesses in 12 months, representing approximately $500MM in revenue. Our approach makes it much more likely that we will meet your expectations and get your BUSINESS SOLD!

▶RESTRUCTURE, REFINANCE & GROWTH: Restructured & Refinanced by reducing debt and operating costs by 70% and brought in additional capital for long term growth.

▶FINANCE: All types of loans, leases, asset based lending; $500K to $500MM from 100+ institutional sources. We are experts in restructuring, refinancing and debt mediation.

SPECIALTIES: Mergers & Acquisitions / Financing / Revenue Growth / Exit Strategy / Manufacturing / Service Industry / Turnarounds / Business Development / Due Diligence / Contract Negotiations / Strategic Planning / Private Equity / Venture Capital / Due Diligence / Business Valuation / Financial Analysis / ReStructure

What three books do you feel are a must that you highly recommend others to read? *The Ultimate Sales Machine* by Chet Holmes, *Getting Things Done* by David Allen and *Solution Selling: Creating Buyers in Difficult Selling Markets* by Michael Bosworth. I tend to focus on and enjoy books that I consider more practical than theoretical.

What will you do differently this year from last year or what do you want more of? It is not what I will do differently, for me, it is what will I do better than last year. I have an annual practice of looking at my calendar and identifying the lowest value 20% of my tasks and finding a way to remove them from my calendar. This year I plan to a) do a better job of identifying those 20% and b) doing this semiannually vs annually. Why, to increase my business while working more efficiently and effectively.

In helping others, is it better to teach them, give them, or show them? A mentor of mine once shared with me the medical school approach to training new doctors which is; "see one, do one teach one." It makes sense, first show someone how to do something, this means you have to have a process and outcome that can be communicated. Second, have that person do one for you while you observe. Third, once they have the process down, have them teach the process to someone new. This approach is highly effective in every environment in which I have ever been involved.

Fred's Favorite Characteristics
Problem Solver, Ethical, Detailed, Visonary

Fred Sussman aka "Maximum Value Creator For Business" M&A ♘ Strategy ♞ Business Growth ♖ Capital ♕ TurnAround ♔ ReStructuring ♔ Consultant ♔ Business Coaching ♔ Data Room ♔ Director ♔ Partner ♜ FSussman@VisionaryCG.com ♟ 314-300-6500 ♕
http://www.visionarycg.com ✓

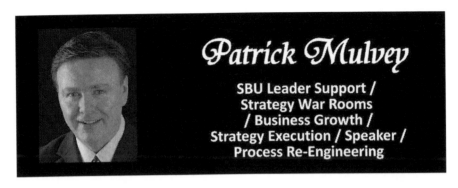

Patrick Mulvey

SBU Leader Support /
Strategy War Rooms
/ Business Growth /
Strategy Execution / Speaker /
Process Re-Engineering

"We are now clearly recognized as thought leaders in strategy and our growth prospects are unprecedented in both traditional and emerging market segments." - Peggy Nelson, Director Systems Development Operation Northrop Grumman Mission Systems

Always fascinated with solving problems, my curiosity took focus at age ten, with my first chemistry set. It led me to pursue chemical engineering to solve more complex process problems. Evolving from technology to products, to marketing, I awakened to the role of processes underlying corporate problems and their solutions; naturally leading to business strategy and the discipline of management consulting.

Today I help leaders of $50M to $500M in size (whether they are independent or subsidiaries of multi-billion-dollar global conglomerates) to clarify their strategy and align their people with the tools and a clear action plan to ensure it gets done.

▶My business model is different: I listen, question, discuss, and then propose a fixed-fee project with deliverables. No billable hours, or open-ended scopes.

▶If you are launching or upgrading your strategy, or you seem to have stalled in implementing it, you have that in common with 80% of today's organizations.

▶We can make your strategy clear, cogent, and compelling. Moreover, we can provide you with the tools to translate it into actions and an accountability process to do it.

Specialties: Helping executives overcome stagnation and slow growth. Most of the reasons have become invisible over time and can easily be identified with a fresh and candid perspective.

What three books do you feel are a must that you highly recommend others to read? *What Customers Want* by Tony Ulwick, explains with technical rigor, exactly how to determine customers' needs. *The Nature of Personal Reality* by Jane Roberts, reveals how our world operates at a spiritual level. *The Liberty Amendments* by Mark Levin, describes exactly how our Constitutional Republic can be restored as to its proper balance at the Federal level.

What movie touched you by its meaning or inspired you? It's really a kids movie, called *The Never Ending Story*. The message reveals how levels of consciousness give expression to dimensions of reality.

Who in your childhood was a major influence that helped shape your life? My 11th grade Social Studies teacher, Mr. George Karadenes, taught me to believe in myself and that I had what it takes to succeed.

What discipline could someone learn from you that would take them to the next level, and how did you develop it? Thinking strategically by learning to see the whole and not just some of the parts.

If you could have any superpower (or be any superhero), what/who would it be and why? As a child, I always wanted to be the Green Lantern because with the Green Lantern's ring, all he needed was the ability to have a clear vision and vivid imagination to create anything. I already have those. I just need the ring.

If there were one problem in the world you could solve, what would it be? I would like to help young people understand what makes the USA an exceptional country and encourage them to extend our intended virtues of liberty, responsibility, and respect for law.

What will you do differently this year from last year or what do you want more of? I must be more mindful that productivity means time spent on my goals, be they personal or professional.

Patrick's Favorite Characteristics
Grateful, Joyous, Trustworthy, Dependable, Honest, Inquisitive

Patrick Mulvey aka "Stratman" - Your Strategist!
Author: "B4 Strategy Know This" & "Strategic Accountability"
Helping clients develop a clear vision, compelling strategy, and the
accountability tools to get it done.
PMulvey@StrategyDone.com 908-391-6010
http://www.strategydone.com
LinkedIn Profile: https://www.linkedin.com/in/patrickmulvey1

Man is not born
to solve the problems
of the universe,
but to find out
what he has to do...
within the limits
of his comprehension.

Johann Wolfgang
von Goethe

Chapter 12
Reinventing Yourself & Beyond

When the voice and the vision on the inside is more profound, and more clear and loud than all opinions on the outside, you've begun to master your life.

--Dr. John Demartini

Dr. John Demartini

International Speaker, Leadership and Performance Specialist. Founder of the Demartini Institute
Houston, Texas | Professional Training & Coaching

Current   The Demartini Institute, Keynote Speaker

Send a message ▾

500+
connections

My Influencers: Dr. John Demartini

We are so lucky to live in this time of technology. We used to say our drive time was our university on wheels. Now we are really mobile with iPods, mp3's, and smartphones. We can connect with every possible media and listen to our education while we are working out, waiting for a client, or sitting on the beach.

A friend told me that since I loved searching for knowledge, I should check out Dr. John Demartini. I looked him up on LinkedIn and saw we shared over 40 connections and three of my favorite groups. Then I saw his LinkedIn articles. That night I went home and looked him up on YouTube. Night after night I watched his presentations, interviews, and snippets. I was fascinated that one of his particular topics was how he spent his life studying billionaires and their values. Every time I listened I heard something different. I was so hooked I had to go see him live.

If your actions inspire others to dream more, learn more, do more and become more, you are a leader.
--John Quincy Adams

Dr Demartini has spoken in over 90 countries and travels 360 days around the world each year. Bazinga! When I looked at his schedule on his website, I saw he was coincidentally going to speak in Santa Monica at the Fairmont. I felt so lucky, like I had put an order into the universe and it delivered for me. Even though I had previously absorbed a wealth of his information on the internet, the evening was a 10. I couldn't write fast enough to record all the brilliance of this genius.

At the event, Dr. John shared that you need to identify what is truly valuable to you. Your life demonstrates your values through how you live. On his web site, I found a free self-evaluation on your values. To become aware of these values, ask yourself what energizes you, how you fill your space, and how you spend your time and money.

There must have been at least 50 different books available at the back of the room. The most impressive was that Dr. J has the largest gratitude book in the world. I learned from John that giving appreciation and gratitude starts you on your journey to wealth.

Consider adding him to your influencer list.

Coaches, Mentors & Role Models

When we develop habits, those habits control our destiny. This is why people who make millions of dollars are willing to pay a coach one thousand dollars a month without thinking anything of it to keep themselves on track, taking the actions they commit to taking.

Building these habits is a lifetime endeavor. That's why one of the best things you can do is hire a coach to keep on track as you build the record that will make you a prime candidate for new jobs. You need this coaching support because it is so easy to get sidetracked when you're not supported by a structure that tells you what to do every day.

One of my favorite people to go to lunch with during events is Kory Minor. I met Kory a few years back and had no idea who he was. At a recent speaking event, we bumped into each other and talked for a few minutes. I realized he was charming, funny, and down to earth.

I asked him, "What did you do in your previous life?"

He responded, "I was a linebacker and special teams player for the San Francisco 49ers."

I was so excited because I'm from the Bay area. As we talked, I asked Kory what he was most proud of in his life. He said that he was a blessed man because he received a full scholarship to Notre Dame University. He played football for the Irish and got an amazing education. We then moved on to Kory's mentor, Les Brown, who coincidentally is one of my mentors and one of my favorite people.

The price of success is hard work, dedication to the job at hand, and the determination that whether we win or lose, we have applied the best of ourselves to the task at hand.
--Vince Lombardi

I asked him, "How and why did you make the transition from football to speaker?"

He thought for a moment and then said, "Everybody gets knocked down and we all have to get back up. Not everybody has an easy childhood and some of us come from the wrong side of the tracks. But everyone fights adversity."

Kory explained that his biggest fear is the fear of failure. He had a strong desire to create his own legacy and a dream of becoming an entrepreneur. Kory is the Founder and CEO of Kory Minor Industries (www.koryminor.com) which is a personal development and training company working with individuals and organizations to "get off the sideline and get into the game." He has written the book *Make a Touchdown of Your Life* and believes that you have greatness inside you. Kory says there are four pieces to the success puzzle:

1. Have a game plan
2. Take action
3. Fight through adversity
4. Be adaptable

Kory sees life as a vessel to help others. He believes that if you have the right play and follow the right steps you can make a touchdown of your life. Kory's big goal is to teach teenagers financial literacy. He believes that smart people use their brains make a difference.

Les Brown is one of my favorite mentors. He has worked with many generations and inspired many people. When you watch Les Brown speak you can feel the energy he generates. He is filled with passion and gives deep, emotional speeches. At one point, I had the opportunity to have dinner with him. A friend invited me to meet up with her and it turns out that her husband was getting private coaching from Les Brown. They invited me to dinner and it was such an honor to have dinner with one of my greatest role models. There were just 10 of us there and it is an experience I will never forget.

How the Internet Changed Opportunities

In today's world, information is at your fingertips. Want to find a place to eat? Search for one and within a minute you will have more choices than you know what to do with.

The internet has also changed the way we learn. We have developed technologies and systems that extend education to a larger group of people. Online classes for people of all ages are becoming more and more popular. Changes are coming so fast with the internet that not only is education available, education companies are finding ways to increase and improve the outcomes that internet education can deliver.

When you believe you can – you can!
--Maxwell Maltz

In 2004 Salman Kahn began posting math tutorial videos on You Tube. From these videos, he developed the Kahn Academy, a carefully structured series of educational videos offering complete curricula originally in math but now in additional subjects as well. He teaches through the videos and shows the power of interactive exercises. He's flipping the current education model and asks teachers to create video lectures the students can watch at home while doing homework in class where they can ask questions and get help.

Leadership is the art of getting someone else to do something you want done because he wants to do it.
--Dwight D. Eisenhower

The teachers that use Kahn's videos are using technology to humanize the classroom. The one-size-fits-all lectures are gone, replaced by students interacting with one another to learn. One of Kahn's biggest supporters in this new form of education is Bill Gates. The Kahn Academy is a non-profit organization with significant funding from the Bill & Melinda Gates Foundation, Ann and John Doer, Lemann Foundation, and Google.

In addition to new ways of learning, students have access to more information than ever before. Projects and reports that used to be taxing have become much simpler due to the internet. Articles and books are online and easily accessible. Knowledge is at everyone's fingertips. You just have to step out and search for it.

Visions & Visualizations

John Assaraf

CEO, PraxisNow | Built 5 Multi-Million Dollar Companies |
Philanthropist | NY Times Best Selling Author

Rancho Santa Fe, California | Professional Training & Coaching

Current	PraxisNow
Previous	RIA Ventures, Inc., IPIX Corporation, RE/MAX of Indiana
Education	Montreal Canada

Send a message   Endorse ▾

500+
connections

In the movie *The Secret*, there's a scene where John Assaraf had just moved into his new home and was unpacking boxes in his office. His son walked in to help him unpack. He pulled a large board with pictures and words pasted on it out of a box. "Wow, my old vision board," he said. "It's been years since I looked at this."

"What's a vision board, Dad?" his son asked.

"A vision board is a place where you put your dreams," he said. "You write down or add photos of the stuff you want to accomplish and it helps you work toward it."

Failure is the opportunity to more intelligently begin again.
-Henry Ford

He opened the box and pulled out the vision board that he had created five years earlier. As he turned the board around his son gasped. There on the board was a photo of the house they had just moved into. Five years earlier, John had put his house on the vision board, and his vision had just come true. What a coincidence.

Recently I stayed at my friend Stephanie's house in Laguna Niguel, California, just south of Los Angeles, for the weekend. When I arrived, she met me at the door and said, "I got you a spot under the stars."

"What do you mean?" I replied.

"I got you a spot under the stars. Follow me." We headed down the hall to an amazing room with huge windows and a soft fluffy bed piled with pillows. I thought, "This is amazing." Then I looked up and saw stars above my head. I thought I was in heaven!

After a night of wonderful dreams in an amazing room under the stars, I woke up refreshed. I looked around and on her bookshelf I saw John Assaraf's book, *The Vision Board Book*. What a coincidence. John Assaraf and I had connected through LinkedIn.

My friend Stephanie arrived and saw me with the book. "I see you got into my books," she said.

"I'm a book nut. I love this book and John Assaraf is one of my connections on LinkedIn." I then shared the story of the vision board and the house with Stephanie.

"I'm in that book," she said.

"No way!" I said.

"I'm in that book," she said again.

Again, I said, "No way!"

"I'm in that book. There's a story about how I trained to compete in the Ironman Competition."

It finally sunk in. My friend Stephanie was actually in this book! She told me the whole story. She had done several triathlons and had just finished a race in Boston. Shortly after that race, she received a call informing her that she had qualified for the Ironman Competition in Hawaii. This worldwide competition has only 1,500 spots available. She had just qualified for one of those spots. They needed one question answered immediately, "Are you in or will you pass?"

An answer right now, she thought, okay, when opportunity knocks just say yes. So she said yes. She had just committed to this event, but then realized she had no idea what she had committed to. What was an Ironman? Where was it? When was it? She had no clue that she had just committed herself to an Ironman competition in Hawaii in 45 days.

Once she figured out that it was a triathlon that included three events, a 2.4-mile swim, a 112-mile bike race, and a 26.2-mile marathon, she realized she had to do something drastic.

If you can get better at your job, you should be an active member of LinkedIn, because LinkedIn should be connecting you to the information, insights, and people to be more effective.
-Reid Hoffman

She had never done anything remotely like this. Most athletes train for the Ironman for a year or two. She had 45 days. So she went to the one person she knew who could help her, a friend who trained athletes on visualization. This friend agreed to help her train for her Ironman and they began with very specific drills and training for both the mind and body. She had to condition her mind to see the end result before she could get her body in shape in 45 days. She focused on seeing herself in the race, seeing her body in condition for the race, and felt herself running the race.

The power of our mind, the biggest muscle we possess, is incredible. She performed a successful Ironman because she stayed focused and trained her mind to get her to where she needed to be physically.

Billion Dollar Mindset

One of my favorite people from *The Secret* is John D. Martini. John mentioned that *The Secret* told a lot of great stories about universal laws but he adds the action steps needed to get to the end in mind. This process is how billionaires make their billions of dollars.

One billionaire he talks about is Warren Buffet. People wonder how successful people become successful. At age 11 Warren Buffet read every book on finance in the Nebraska State Library in Omaha. No wonder Warren Buffet is worth $50 billion dollars. This Billionaire Circle and includes members such as Buffet, Richard Branson, Donald Trump, Sara Blakely, (the youngest female billionaire), Bill Gates, and Steve Jobs. Even if you don't have the desire to become a billionaire, the success principles they use will lead you to success.

Before 1954, nobody had run a mile in under four minutes. Many people, including doctors, believed it was impossible for a human being to run that fast. Roger Bannister ignored all of the naysayers and in 1954 broke the four-minute barrier. Since then, over 20,000 people have reached that seemingly unreachable goal.

Les Brown says that everything is possible. Everything you need is already inside you, waiting to be used. When you operate out of your imagination and not your memory, you will see possibilities everywhere and will be able to act on them.

Think about what people are doing on Facebook today. They're keeping up with their friends and family, but they're also building an image and identity for themselves, which in a sense is their brand. They're connecting with the audience that they want to connect to.

--Mark Zuckerberg

Why it is important to me to show you that my awareness to the billionaire circle is twofold?

1. I didn't know that there are over 1,645 billionaires. Did you? Awareness is the first step to learning everything including yourself.

2. When you played the "I am" game (your character traits), you helped yourself get clear of who you are so you can authentically share with other in order for them to get to know you better. With millionaires and billionaires their characteristics and skills will help you to see, if you see greatness in others you can see it in yourself. What other possibilities could this create for you?

Here are a few billionaires

Giorgio Armani- Fashion Designer

Jeff Bezos- Amazon

Liliane Bittencourt- L'Oreal

Sara Blakley- Spanx (youngest female billionaire)

Michael Bloomberg- Bloomberg LP (stock market)
Donald Bren- Real Estate
Sergey Brin- Google
Warren Buffet- Berkshire Hathaway
Michael Dell- Dell computers
Larry Ellison-Oracle
Bill Gates- Microsoft
Reid Hoffman- LinkedIn
Steve Jobs- Apple
Phil Knight- Niki
Eric Lefkosky- Groupon
Forrest Mars- Candy
Dietrich Mateschitz- Red Bull
Howard Schultz- Starbucks
Donald Trump- Television, Real Estate
Christy Walton- Walmart
Ty Warner- Beanie Babies
Mark Zuckerberg- Facebook

Think Tank & Mastermind

Imagine that you just took a trip around the world with eight of the smartest people in the world. Would you see things from a different perspective?

I met Roger Salam at a Tony Robbins event 30 years ago and knew without a shadow of doubt that he was a difference maker.

As years passed I decided to make a list of people I had met back then since I wondered where they were.

One by one found them. When Roger reappeared, I was not surprised that he had become an international speaker and author, worked directly with Tony Robbins, and did 3,700 talks. As founder of The Winner Circle runs the most unique mastermind event in the world at a 38,000 square-foot mansion.

One of the challenges in networking is everybody thinks it's making cold calls to strangers. Actually, it's the people who already have strong trust relationships with you, who know you're dedicated, smart, and a team player, who can help you.
-- Reid Hoffman

Recently, I was part of an all the star lineup and got to speak at icon event with my long-lost friend Roger "Wajed" Salam. Roger says that positioning is key when forming a mastermind group. You look at the end result you want to achieve as a whole to create your vision and mission. Individual goals may very but your core values and principles must align.

Roger says a core 100 people who are aligned can mastermind together and influence millions. My favorite quotes are, "Who you hang with, who you associate with, and who you listen to will determine your destiny" and "None of us is as smart as all of us."

Amazing Grace, a Pondering Thought

Amazing Grace by John Newton is an amazing song sung in hundreds of churches all over the world. Yet most people are not aware of the deep sorrow attached to it, the many lives that were lost, and the stories behind them. The even more astounding but extremely thought-provoking paradox is how we... you... me... each one of us... can change or be difference makers.

In the mid eighteenth century, John Newton, age 22, was a slave trader exporting human lives from West Africa to South Carolina on his own slave ship. One night he had a dramatic faith experience during a storm at sea. Following that storm he gave his life to God and began to read spiritual books and pray. He continued to run his slave ships, making three more voyages. Two days before his fourth voyage was to set sail, a mysterious illness temporarily paralyzed him. He never made the fourth journey.

That experience changed his life, which changed his thinking. He became a pastor who opposed the slave trade. In 1788 he met William

Wilberforce, an influential Member of Parliament, and began to mentor him on the slave trade. The two men collaborated in a campaign to outlaw the slave trade. In 1807 the once sinner Newton along with Wilberforce and their colleagues prevailed when Parliament voted to outlaw the slave trade in Britain. He almost single-handedly abolished slavery. The sinner became one of the most influential humanitarians of his time and the ripple effect of his actions changed the world.

Most of us fail to question how it happens that people can create such devastating life events as slavery and how we can prevent such moral failings in the future. John Newton was born into the slave trade. At the age of 11 in 1743, he went to sea with his father to Jamaica as a slave master. He became a midshipman, was demoted for trying to desert, and then returned to West Africa on another slave ship.

Many people go through tragedies and hardships that other people who haven't walked in their shoes cannot understand. These others are filled with judgment and criticism because they take their everyday freedom for granted and do not realize what it took for the person they criticize to get where they are.

We all have been involved in judgment and criticism and even condemnation toward another person because we believe they should or should not have done something.

Dr. Wayne Dyer shared in his program *Wishes Fulfilled* that as soon as he let go his self-defeating inflections, he created miracles in his life. We are all just doing what we know how to do. (paraphrased) "We must let go of any thoughts of judgment, criticism or condemnation. We are all God's children," he says.

Here are This Chapter's Business Consultant Influencers

As you read these profiles, look for possible referrals for your needs.

Is there something in their story you connect with?

Could you gain a new idea or insight for your business or career?

Who do you know or who do they know that can help both of you?

If you needed help or wanted to buy a product, what would it be?

How do you follow up when you meet someone?

When people view your profile, how do you want them to feel?

Do your tribes line up so you could be Power Partners?

What are your favorite questions to ask in an introductory call?

Risk comes from not knowing what you are doing. ~ Warren Buffett

I started writing computer programs in Basic on a Commodore 64 when I was 8 years old. I recycled bottles and cans and mowed lawns to buy more computer games on cassettes. At 12, I knew I hated door to door sales, so I donated my own earnings directly to the school, so I didn't have to sell magazines, candy, etc., to my neighbors. I funded my college and 1st home by investing student loans into Janus and 20th Century mutual funds.

Today I help successful business owners and entrepreneurs including doctors & attorneys, real estate investors, corporate executives, top sales performers in their industry and especially people who are growing & selling successful businesses be able to directly access wealth building strategies previously only available to institutions & the mega wealthy

▶ Caliber:The Wealth Development Company is an Inc 500/5000 company for 4 years in a row, as the Director of Private Client Group where his primarily role is to drive revenue and increase shareholder value.

▶ Collaborated with successful serial entrepreneurs to start and build an entrepreneurial community called Eliances: Where Entrepreneurs Align. We deliver the resources that all business owner needs to go from an idea to a growing, profitable company by bringing together the people, processes and connections required to be a thriving business

▶As a founding member of the management team of the Royal Palms Resort and Spa in sunny Phoenix, Arizona, Brion honed his customer service and management skills to enable Caliber Hospitality to become a first class owner/operator of full service, limited service and boutique hotels.

Specialties: Financing / Revenue Growth / Exit Strategy / Sustainability / Hospitality Industry / Turnarounds / Business Development / Due Diligence / Commercial Real Estate / Strategic Planning / Private Equity / Venture Capital / Entrepreneurship / Financial Planning/Advisory Board/Board of Directors/ Non-Profits

If there were one problem in the world you could solve, what would it be? Food and water insecurity - We believe that through shared knowledge and collaboration that the will and the technology to solve many issues related global sustainability with air, food, energy and water has already been created and exists. When I am able to create and implement automation and systems to allow myself and Caliber: The Wealth Development Company to be able connect with and interact with more investors seeking wealth, I will have the freedom to pursue these greater pursuits with our partners in www.VerdeExchange.com

What do you wish you spent more time doing? Being involved in philanthropic activities and not limiting it to donations of time and money but being able to implement proven strategies, technologies, techniques and investment strategies for charitable organizations so that they can thrive and become sustaining What prevents you from doing that now? Currently building up multiple entrepreneurial and wealth building systems to allow freedom to pursue passions

Who now is a Mentor, Coach or Strategist that is on your advisory council? David Cogan our founder of Eliances:Where Entrepreneurs Align

Brion's Favorite Characrteristics
Innovative, charitable, entrepreneurial

Brion Crum aka "The Human Link". Innovating in Financial Technologies & Building Wealth for Others Through Entrepreneurship & Real Estate Investing ▶ Brion.Crum@CaliberCo.com ◀ & ▶ 480-349-6573 ◀
▶ www.InvestWithBrion.com www.CaliberCo.com
https://twitter.com/brioncrum; https://www.linkedin.com/in/brioncrum/

Glen Depke

**Anti Aging / Hormone Balance /
Inflammation / Brain Fog /
Food Allergies /
Speaker & Author**

"Whether you think you can, or you think you can't--you're right."
Henry Ford

When I was 17 I experienced my first grand mal seizure. When I woke up after it stopped I felt like I'd been run over by a truck. I started taking anticonvulsant medication, but my doctor was never able to find out what caused the seizure. Even while on the medication I experienced additional seizures. I took things into my own hands and began researching my medication and condition. I found out that the medicine I was taking could could cause permanent neuro degeneration.

Armed with determination I was able to help myself get better by understanding and addressing the underlying triggers. I and now seizure free without medication.

Today I'm a Traditional Naturopath and own Depke Wellness. I'm trained in the use of non-invasive tools to bring balance to the body with the goal of "allowing" true healing. I look at the body physically, mentally, emotionally and spiritually to understand fundamental imbalances. It's my goal to empower individuals to reach their fullest potential on every level desired.

► Professional Woman who are concerned with Hormone Balance, Stress Release, Brain Health and feeling and looking young. I can help you if you've been burning the candle at both ends.

► Pain Management for Executives. Is your pain or lack of energy keeping you from doing the things you love?

► Stressed Out and Overwhelmed on a continuous basis? It's not just what you need to do at your business, but it's what you need to do on a personal basis. If no matter what you do nothing seems to make a difference, I can help.

SPECIALTIES: Anti-Aging / Hormone Balance / Inflammation / Brain Fog / Food Allergies / Pain Management / Feeling at Ease and Energetic / Want more Energy / Reduce Stress / Traditional Naturopath / Speaker & Author

What will you do differently this year from last year or what do you want more of? This year I am going to spent far more quality and fun time with my wife. We have been in such a "go mode" with our business since moving to SoCal and it's time to step back a bit and smell the roses.

What discipline could someone learn from you? Anyone can learn to allow your innate healing ability to occur by integrating your functional, mental, emotional and vibrational health. Addressing these components holistically allows for your natural balance and healing to create a new you.

What subject or argument most stirs your emotions, why? The thought that all we have to do it take a prescription drug and all our problems goes away truly stirs me up. While I do not bash conventional medicine, there is a time and a place, most people with chronic ailments need lifestyle and functional health assistance to allow the body to recover.

On what topic at parties would you really like to "get into it"? I absolutely love to talk about health and could do so for hours. It is also important for me to meet the people in my conversation where they're at. Making health simple in conversation is my gift.

When "winning someone over" do you think facts or emotions carry the day? Both all the way. Just driving emotion is incomplete and can even be manipulative. Adding in the facts with the emotions provides the balance needed for most to be on board. I also like to think of it as becoming a team, rather than winning someone over.

In helping others, is it better to teach them, give them, or show them? If feel that all of these can play a role depending on the individual and you have to have all of these tools ready for any given moment. When I am working with my clients, the bigger focus is on teaching and showing, yet every once in a while you have to simply "give" something to help create that shift or push they may need.

What movie makes you cry, every time you see it? The end of *It's a Wonderful Life*. Tears of joy stream down my face every time I see that movie. I wish we all had the opportunity to see how our lives impact others.

Glen's Favorite Characteristics:
Compassionate, Good Listener, Knowledgeable, Passionate, Persistent, Believe in My Clients, Determined

Glen Depke aka Your Stress Hormone Expert "Feel Young Again"
♛ Anti Aging ♚ Hormone Balance ♛ Inflammation ♚ Pain and Stress Management
♟ glen@depkewellness.com ♟ 708-302-3665 ♛
www.DepkeWellness.com ✓

Ted Mortarotti

**Real Estate Syndicators
at Equidyne Partners, Inc.**

*"Your investments should be a reflection of your Goals, Dreams &
Desires" Ted Mortarotti*

Can you imagine Wisconsin at 5 am with the weather 30 below zero? I started my entrepreneurial journey at 7 years old as a Pony Express delivery boy. Not only did I roll, wrap and deliver, I collected. My Dad says, "If you want money you have to earn it."

Today Equidyne Partners helps investors beat Wall Street returns through group investment (syndication) in the Apartment World. We all want to be involved in something bigger than ourselves.Equidyne Partners has a profitable niche in the apartment business in renovations. We scour national markets for well-located, underperforming properties, outdated or poorly maintained facilities and/or mismanaged rent rolls. Out of this stew comes profits.

▶ Many of our clients start out with only their 401-K Plans. They had invested in mutual funds with miniscule returns of just 2-3% after broker's fees. By transferring their funds to a "self-directed" real estate account they have exceeded their expectations.

▶ Are you tired of tenants & toilets? Equidyne Partners, Inc. is a syndication company with 30 years of leveraging your dollars, lowering your maintenance and liability. We search for unique opportunities to accelerate equity growth!!!

SPECIALTIES: Real Estate Strategist / Syndicator / Multi Units 100-500 / Renovation / Investor / Changed Use / Exchanges / Private Placements / Broker Referrals / Property Management / CrowdFunding

Who in your childhood was a major influence that helped shape your life? My dad would say "If you want money you have to go earn it" I started my entrepreneurship at 7 years old with a paper route in Wisconsin with 30 below zero . Not only did I roll & wrap, deliver I collected. "neither rain - nor snow"

What will you do differently this year from last year? Not much, Family first, buy only investments that fit my formula, higher the right people and be grateful every day.

What discipline could someone learn from you? Know how what you want works, study it, learn from successors, keep the end in mind, but have check marks all the way in the process and keep humble learn from everyone & everything in the process

In helping others, is it better to teach them, give them, or show them? I feel that is based on circumstances, for someone homeless is just give with no expectations. In work related I found I have to show them multiple times and with children I do my best to lead by example.

If there were one problem in the world you could solve, what would it be? In business so many people fail that have good intentions, but they don't have the right model or leadership to follow. In addition, they need a way to have sustainability to get there.

What do you wish you spent more time doing? My Family, my wife & our children, I can never spend too much time with them

Ted's Favorite Characteristics
Family First, Organized, Trustworthy, Dedicated, Numbers Guy, Responsible

Ted Mortarotti aka "The Insider Investor"
Unlocking Hidden Potential Through Profit Making Renovations
▶TM@EquidynePartners.com◀ ▶818-612-1066◀

Printed in Great Britain
by Amazon